The Industrial Windmill
in Britain

THE
INDUSTRIAL WINDMILL
IN BRITAIN

Roy Gregory

PHILLIMORE

2005

Published by
PHILLIMORE & CO. LTD
Shopwyke Manor Barn, Chichester, West Sussex, England

ISBN 1 86077 334 6

Printed and bound in Great Britain by
THE CROMWELL PRESS
Trowbridge, Wiltshire

Previous page: Whiting Mill at Stoneferry, Hull, as it stood in 1889. The mill was originally built between 1755 and 1790. (See illustration 10.)

Contents

List of Illustrations

Preface and Acknowledgements

The traditional windmill has been around in Britain for nearly one thousand years, grinding wheat into flour for our daily bread and, in some parts of the country, pumping water off low-lying land. These aspects of the windmill's story have been most ably covered by a number of books, starting with the work of Bennett and Elton in the 1890s, through to the definitive work on corn mill technology by Rex Wailes and the range of books which deal with individual counties. Most of these works give passing mention to other uses, for example, crushing oil seed, sawing timber and grinding snuff. But this aspect of the windmill's capability has never been examined in detail.

There is certainly a story to be told. Some time ago, whilst researching the history of the Hull millwrights, Messrs Norman and Smithson (1780-1831), it became very apparent to me that the windmill had played a significant part in the development of the industrial base in several towns and merited further investigation.

I have attempted to compile a list of known windmills which were used, neither for milling grain nor pumping water for land drainage schemes, but by the entrepreneurial merchants and manufacturers of the day, for the extraction and processing of raw materials, the manufacture of commodities, and the transport of such items. The results are contained in the following pages, in which I first describe the various tasks these mills performed and then attempt to analyse why wind power was chosen in preference to other contemporary power sources.

To date I have found references to 262 windmills which meet these criteria. There were certainly more than this, as I have come across references to the use of wind power but without specific examples being quantified, particularly in relation to mines and salterns. I estimate this figure represents some seven per cent of all the wind-powered cornmills working on the British mainland during the period 1800 to 1850. A modest but, as I hope to show, important percentage.

In the following chapters, the various uses have been organised under chapter headings which to some extent is an arbitrary grouping. But I hope this will make the subject easier for the reader to assimilate.

I have sought and benefited from information from various people, particularly fellow members of the Mills Section of The Society for the Protection of Ancient Buildings, and I would like particularly to express my thanks to Dr Michael Lewis, Stephen Buckland, Richard Crumblehome, Peter Dolman, Peter Filby, Alan Gifford, Ann Gregory, William Hill, Kenneth Major, Gerallt Nash, Don Paterson, Jon Sass, Michael Short, Geoffrey Starmer, Alan Stoyel, Laurence Turner, Martin

Watts, Catherine Whalen; Tony Carr (Shropshire Record and Research Service), John Howell (English Ceramic Circle), Mrs A. Rix (Norfolk Windmills Trust), Jason Morden (Nottinghamshire County Council), Hazel Ramsden (King's Lynn Library), Sue Richards (Laing Art Gallery) and the staff of a number of other local history libraries and county record offices.

I do, of course, take full responsibility for any errors or omissions, and for the views and opinions expressed.

Finally, I have included several illustrations the copyright of which is either in private ownership or the ownership of a public archive, art gallery or library. The names of such owners are set out under the respective illustrations and I would like to acknowledge their courtesy in permitting me to reproduce such illustrations.

ROY GREGORY

1

'The Romantic Windmill'?

'The Romantic Windmill' was the title used on publicity material, advertising an exhibition of paintings assembled by the Hove Museum and Art Gallery in 1993 and subsequently displayed at the Walker Gallery in Lincoln and Gainsborough's House at Sudbury. The full title of the exhibition was 'The Windmill in British Art from Gainsborough to David Cox 1750-1803' and the significance of the publicity title becomes apparent when one reads the background notes included in the very informative catalogue. The word 'romantic' relates to the artists, not the windmills.

The catalogue editor points out that the windmill was used by the romantic artists not simply to produce a picturesque painting. The windmill was a direct link between the mechanical devices of man and the natural world around him. It drew attention to the sky, to the wind and to a concept central to the romantic movement, namely that nature is constantly changing. To illustrate the point he refers to a painting by the Dutch artist, J. van Ruisdael, which seems to have greatly influenced John Constable (a miller's son), entitled simply 'Winter Landscape'. It shows a wintry scene with fields and trees covered with frosty snow and includes two windmills, one with sails set, the other with bare poles, each pointing in a different direction. Overhead the clouds are opening from the direction in which the working mill is pointing, and the sun is beginning to appear. Constable deduced that the picture told the story of an approaching thaw after a cold night. The fact that it was morning emerged from the different position of the windmills, that with bare poles being in the position it was left by the miller when he finished work at the end of the previous day, the other, in which the miller is making an early start, having been turned to face the new direction from which the wind was blowing. To interpret the story it was, of course, necessary to understand the basics of how a windmill worked and many artists took pains to depict the various parts of the mills with great accuracy.

Unfortunately not all artists painted the mill with such accuracy. Some depict them as quite rickety affairs in order to give the picture a rustic feel. This concept of the romantic windmill has left a legacy which perhaps obscures the true place of the windmill in industrial history, and brings us to an alternative way in which the shortened title to the exhibition may well have been understood by the casual observer. There is no doubt that many people see the windmill as a quaint and romantic feature in the rural landscape, part of the 'Merrie England' syndrome but, whereas everybody is entitled to enjoy a subject from whatever angle they choose, by viewing the windmill in this way, and this way only, the observer is missing its true value. The traditional windmill was, and still is, an engine, one that can deliver power for various uses, and throughout history this has been its purpose. If one takes the definition of a machine as 'a contrivance for doing work more easily', this fits a windmill equally as well as a watermill, a steam engine or the internal combustion engine.

Down the years, most writers on the history and mechanics of windmills have concentrated on the use of this wind-powered engine to crush grain or drain agricultural land, which certainly have been the major uses. But these are not the sole uses. The windmill is made up of two elements, that part of the structure which catches the wind and that part of the structure which does the work, e.g. in the case of the corn mill, the grinding and dressing machinery. Indeed the term windmill is really a shorthand form of the full title, i.e. wind-powered corn mill. There is no reason why the structure should not be fitted with machinery to do some other task. This did happen, and it is with these happenings that this book is concerned.

Having introduced the concept of two elements, it is perhaps desirable to say a few words about the engine, that part of the windmill which catches the energy in the wind and converts it into useable mechanical power.

The method of catching the wind is the sail, the commonest arrangement being to have four sails turning in a more or less vertical plane, fixed to a horizontal shaft (the windshaft). Each sail has a surface presented to the wind at an angle, as a result of which the path of the wind is diverted thus creating what the modern aerodynamicists call lift. This lift causes the sail to move and, as the sails are fixed to a central point – the windshaft – the only direction in which the sail can move is to turn about the windshaft, causing the windshaft to produce a rotary motion. The earliest sail used in Western Europe is referred to as the common sail, a very simple arrangement which comprised a rectangular lattice framework over which a canvas sheet was spread, held at the inner end of the sail frame on an iron rail running the full width of the sail. By means of ropes called pointing lines, the canvas could be rolled up so as to cut off the outer corner to a greater or lesser degree according to the strength of the wind. Each sail had to be set or furled by hand, one at a time, and for this purpose each sail had to be brought round to its lowest position in turn. On a wet and stormy day this could be a very unpleasant operation and in the case of those windmills with a gallery or stage around the tower, some 20 to 30 feet up in the air, at times extremely hazardous. It is unlikely that the practical miller saw the operation as romantic! From the 1750s onwards, major improvements to the design of sails appeared and these will be explained at relevant points in the text, as will attempts to use sails turning in a horizontal plane.

Unfortunately, only in a few places does the wind blow constantly from one direction; consequently the engine must be constructed in such a way as to enable the operator to keep the vertical sails facing into wind, generally referred to as 'winding' the mill (pronounced win-ding, not winding as in winding a clock). The original method of winding a mill was one which causes modern engineers to shake their heads in disbelief. It was achieved by constructing a large 'shed' (the buck) which held both the engine (i.e. the sails) and the machinery – in the case of a corn mill the millstones and any supplementary equipment. A hole was left in the floor of the buck and the entire structure was mounted on an upright post which came up through the hole, having a pintle at its top end which fitted into a smaller hole in a substantial transverse beam (the crown tree) on which, in effect, the buck was suspended in the air. Usually the post was kept upright by four diagonal beams (quarter bars) which were held in place by two further beams (cross trees) between opposing quarter bars, which crossed at the centre and also served to locate the bottom end of the post and maintain it in an upright position. There was also, in many cases, a collar around the post at the point where the top end of the quarter bars were mortised into it, which might also give some support to the buck, particularly when the structure started to sag with age. At the opposite end to the sails, a long pole (the tail pole) extended downwards at an angle, acting as a lever, by means of which the miller could rotate the entire buck to keep the sails facing into wind. In some cases a winch was attached to the tail pole, with the loose end of the rope attached to posts spaced around the perimeter of the turning circle; in extreme cases a donkey might be harnessed to the tail pole. It will be readily appreciated that considerable skill was required by the builder, to ensure that the buck was correctly balanced.

In some cases the framework supporting the buck was left open; the mill was therefore described as an open trestle mill. In other cases the framework was enclosed in a circular or multi-sided structure (the roundhouse), with a conical roof which had its apex underneath the buck; a variant, found generally in the area of the country which lies roughly north-east of Birmingham, has the roof of the roundhouse attached to the buck and rotates with it.

A development of the standard post mill was the 'hollow post mill'. As its name suggests, a hole was drilled down the centre of the main post to take a shaft which could drive machinery in the roundhouse. This arrangement appeared first in Holland (the wip mill), where it was used by drainage engineers to drive pumps which lifted water out of the polders. In this case the only element in the buck was the engine, i.e. the sails and the windshaft which, by way of a pair of gear wheels, drove the vertical shaft which passed down the post. At the foot of the vertical shaft a second pair of gear wheels drove the scoop wheel.

From this arrangement it soon became apparent that a much stronger structure could be built by reducing what had been the buck to simply a gear box, now called the cap, and placing any machinery to be driven in the round house, which could be raised in height. Thus we have the alternative type of mill, the smock mill. This type evolved in Holland, where it was made of timber, and was introduced into England in the late 16th century. By the 18th century English millwrights had started to replace the timber body of the mill with the local vernacular material, brick or, less commonly, local building stone. Thus the brick-built windmill, its body having battered sides i.e. being in the shape of a truncated cone, became the standard for most of the country. Early advertisements often refer to these structures as 'a brick built smock mill', giving a clear indication of their derivation. The descriptive name of 'smock mill' is still used when referring to a tower mill built of timber, whilst a mill built of brick or stone is referred to simply as a tower mill. Mechanically the two structure are identical. It must be mentioned that there are examples of small cylindrical tower mills, found particularly around the Mediterranean, France and south-west England but, although the early builders of the battered tower mill must have been aware of these cylindrical structures, it is not directly descended from them.

Unlike the standard post mill, the tower mill provides a complete separation between the 'engine' and the 'machinery'; in effect the engine is totally confined to the cap, while the machinery and working areas are contained within the tower. This is an important factor, as it gives the millwright considerably more flexibility in the layout of the machinery, without any problems relating to balance. It also makes it much simpler to remove machinery used for one purpose and replace it with machinery for a different purpose, as required. The tower is a much more stable structure than the post mill and, if damage does occur due to adverse weather conditions, the damage is likely to be less catastrophic.

For winding the tower mill, the main frame of the cap rests on an iron ring (the curb) fixed to the top of the brickwork, located by horizontal centring wheels. In the first tower mills, like post mills, the cap was winded by a tail pole, and in the larger mills, with a bracing framework. Ultimately winding became automatic by using the fantail, a mini set of sails set at the opposite end of the cap from, and at right angles to, the main sails, which reacted to wind direction by rotating the cap to keep the sails facing into wind. The evolution from hand winding by tail pole to automatic winding by fantail will be explained later at relevant points.

Having established the windmill as a power source or engine, it is appropriate at this stage to examine how much power it could produce or, more correctly, how much of the power of nature it could convert to a useable form of power. And how this output compares with other sources of power.

In the case of the windmill we have very little hard information. The highest recorded figure known to the author relates to a Dutch windmill turning in a 25mph breeze, which it is claimed produced 55hp. This figure must be regarded as exceptional and certainly not applicable to English windmills. An advertisement in 1828 for the sale of Berney Arms Mill, in which it is described as 'a very power-ful mill', claimed that it could produce 24hp. At the other end of the scale, the leading engineer of his day, John Smeaton, claimed one of his mills produced $3\,^2/_3$ hp, which seems a bit on the low side. In the 17th century, a Dutch millwright named Simon Stevin tackled the problem from the opposite end, by calculating the work done, which seems a practical approach. On this basis he concluded that a polder mill produced 10hp.

One of the 17th-century engineers' handbooks gives power requirements for various items of machinery. It advises that a pair of 4ft 6ins millstones would require 5hp and from this figure it seems likely that the best English windmills, with four pairs of stones and supplementary machinery, would need to produce between 15 and 20hp.

Turning now to water power, it must be recognised that the windmill cannot match the water wheel, which has always been the preferred power source. It is likely that at the start of the 18th century the average output of wooden water wheels was in the region of 5 to 7 hp, but by the first decade of the 19th century some very powerful wheels had emerged. For example, at Strutt's Mill at Belper, the first wheel installed in 1804 was rated at 130hp and a second wheel, added a few years later by Hewes, was rated at 80hp. There can be no doubt that by the start of the 19th century the water wheel had become a highly efficient mechanism for converting water power into useable mechanical power.

But water power had an Achilles' heel, namely its geographical inflexibility and, as with all natural power sources, its dependence on the vagaries of nature. Nevertheless, where water power was available, it continued in use well into the 19th century and in the case of Yorkshire textile industry, into the twentieth.

The real competition for the windmill was from steam power. The Newcomen atmospheric engine had been around for most of the 18th century. John Farey, relying upon calculations made by Smeaton in 1779, lists the power ratings of what he describes as 15 large engines used in the Cornish metal mines, which ranged from 29hp to 15hp, with an average of 20hp over all fifteen. Wider use of the Newcomen-type engine was restricted because the engine simply produced a reciprocating motion which was quite adequate to drive pumps to de-water mines, the purpose for which it was invented, but it could not produce a satisfactory rotary motion which was required to drive other machinery. To overcome this difficulty the arrangement known as the water-returning engine was devised: the machinery was driven by a water wheel and a Newcomen pumping engine was used to lift water from the tail race back into the mill pond or, in some more extreme cases, to lift water from a stream into a header tank over the water wheel.

In fact, many Newcomen engines seem to have been used in this way. The water-returning engine was used fairly extensively around Manchester, to power early cotton mills, although in some cases the water was pumped by the earlier Savery device. These devices were built by a local engineer called Wrigley, whose engines had quite a following as the capital cost was less than that of other engines, particularly those built by Boulton & Watt. There is, however, some dispute as to whether they were less expensive to run!

This brings us nicely to the steam engine which eventually produced rotary motion, the Boulton & Watt double acting rotary engine, patents for which were taken out between 1781 and 1785. Rather surprisingly, there is some confusion as to the numbers and power rating of these engines. Lord, writing in 1923, states that, before 1800, 318 Boulton & Watt engines were built, with an average rating of 16hp. Unfortunately, Lord's figures have been challenged from time to time and it seems possible that Boulton & Watt may have built up to 133 more engines than those found by Lord, raising the average power rating to 25hp. The surprising implication of this is, of course, that somehow Lord missed some of the firm's larger engines. It must, however, be noted that, so far as the Boulton & Watt engines fitted with the sun and planet gear between 1781 (the date of the patent) and 1802 were concerned, the firm's order book shows that over two-thirds were rated at 15hp or less.

Having achieved a satisfactory rotary motion, there were still problems facing investors, the first being that the steam engine was more expensive to build and more expensive to operate than the windmill. Two examples, which will be

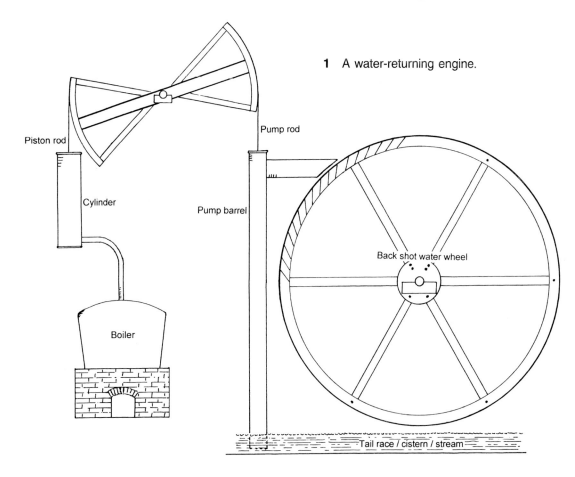

1 A water-returning engine.

explained more fully in later chapters, quite specifically illustrate this point. First, in 1785, a paper mill was opened in Hull, powered by one of the Boulton & Watt double acting rotary beam engines. In 1796, a local firm of millwrights built a second paper mill, powered by wind. Four years later the steam-powered paper mill was out of business. The second example occurred at the Parys Mountain Copper Mine, in Anglesey, where a Cornish beam engine was erected at one of the shafts, to pump water, raise ore and transport men. By the mid-19th century the economics of the mine had deteriorated, so, in order to save costs, in 1878 the company erected a five-sail windmill to supplement the steam engine, which was connected to the machinery by some two hundred feet of flat rods. The windmill proved highly successful, saving considerable costs on coal, and carried on working into the 20th century.

There was a second problem regarding James Watt and his engines, in that he assiduously protected his patent and in doing so effectively prevented any further development of the steam engine, in particular the use of higher pressure steam. The Boulton & Watt engine of 1800 was little different from that of 1785. And we know that in the 1790s Richard Murdoch, a foreman at the Boulton & Watt factory, designed a steam carriage using high pressure steam but was dissuaded from taking it any further by Matthew Boulton. To be fair, it can be said that one reason for this reluctance was the unreliability of some boilers to withstand higher steam pressures.

It was not until the expiry of Watt's patents in 1800 that these impediments disappeared and engines with high pressure steam started to be developed, resulting eventually in smaller and less expensive steam engines being built and equally enabling very large engines to be built to power large mills and heavy engineering plant.

To conclude on the question of power up to 1800, the position with regard to the steam engine, in the context of the present subject, can be summed up as follows. It must be accepted that Boulton & Watt could make engines which produced significantly more power than the English windmill. But there was a demand for power units well within the range of the windmill. Consequently in those areas where the wind resource was suitable, the windmill could meet the demand for such power requirements, and at a significantly lower cost than steam power.

The critical question therefore, relating to the application of wind power, is in which areas of the country is the wind source suitable? It is generally estimated that a traditional windmill will run steadily in a 15mph wind and the best performance can probably be obtained with a wind speed around 20mph. But this is only half the story, as, for a site to be economically viable, the wind must blow at these speeds for a significant percentage of the year. This subject has received considerable attention from modern engineers interested in the use of wind power to generate electricity, and isopleth maps have been produced showing such areas. However, because 18th- and 19th-century millwrights did not have access to such information, it is not intended to explore this matter here. There are no counties in England where wind power has not been used at some time in the past. Such use is certainly more common in some counties than others, the principal areas being East Yorkshire, Lincolnshire, East Anglia, Kent, Sussex, the Fylde and Anglesey. Whereas today's engineers have to be very selective when siting wind turbines, there were fewer limitations on millwrights who wished to obtain 15 or 20hp from the wind.

2

Crushing Oil Seed

The oldest industrial use of wind power for manufacturing products in the UK is the crushing of seed to extract oil, the commonest seeds being rape (also called cole), linseed (from flax) and hemp. The latter two were also grown for their fibre. The oil was used from early times for lamps and the treatment of wool but by the 16th century it was used also to make soap. During the 18th century oil became a vital commodity, being used to lubricate the expanding range of new machinery and to make paint for the numerous metal structures which began to appear.

Rape is an indigenous crop and its production was boosted because it was suitable as a first crop on lands in various parts of eastern England reclaimed through land drainage schemes. The seed crushing industry was to acquire considerable economic significance. By the early 17th century, Britain was producing sufficient oil seed to satisfy internal demand, with a surplus available for export (to Holland and northern France) in the form of seed and cakes (the residue after the oil had been extracted). So much so that in 1643 the Exchequer considered it worthwhile to impose excise duties on the production of oil. During the 18th century, imported seed started to appear and Customs and Excise duties were imposed to protect the home producers. Nevertheless the importation of seed gathered pace, no doubt made necessary because, as the drained marshes were consolidated, less and less oil seed was grown, so that by the end of the 18th century virtually none was grown in Britain.

Harold Brace (*History of Seed Crushing in Great Britain*) suggests that the earliest reference to an oil mill in Britain (as distinct from a reference to an oil merchant) occurs in 1381, when a licence was granted by the lord of the manor for an oil mill to be built at Crowle on the Humber estuary. There is then a gap until 1525 when an oil mill in Hull is mentioned in a will. In neither of these cases is the power source specified but, as water power was not common along the Humber estuary, it is reasonably certain that the mill would have been powered by either wind power or horse power.

Mills powered by the ubiquitous horse were used for crushing a variety of materials, some of which are illustrated by W.H. Pyne in his *Delineation of the Arts, Crafts, Manufacture etc of Great Britain* published in 1808. The basic structure comprised a circular base or pan, dependent upon the material to be crushed, in the centre of which was a sturdy upright shaft, with a bearing at its foot and supported at its upper end by a roof beam, if in a building, or a framework if not.

At a high point a beam extended horizontally from the upright shaft to a point beyond the limit of the base where it held a frame to which a horse could be hitched. A lower and shorter horizontal shaft held a circular stone mounted on its edge. Thus the horse walked in a circle to 'roll' the stone round the base or pan. A similar, but much lighter, arrangement was used until recent times to crush apples in the cider-making districts and examples can still be seen in these areas.

It is not until 1657 that we know for certain that wind power was used to drive oil mills in the Humber area. Brace records that a traveller in the Isle of Axholme (along the Humber estuary): '... passed by four windmills, used for bruising of rape seed, and the making of oyle thereof, which Rapeseed flourisheth much in this rich fenny country, now that it is drained'.

The report does not indicate the type of machinery used in these windmills but we are more fortunate that in 1696 a visitor to the Fens described the machinery in a wind-powered oil mill in the following way:

> Between Spalding and Crowland grow large quantities of Rapum Sylv. (called cole seed) whereof they make Oyl, by breaking it between two great black Marble Stones of near a Tun weight, one standing Perpendicularly on the other (they come out of Germany) in Mills, called Oyl-Mills: some go with sails, and serve to Dreyn the Fens, and are called engines, being of good use, and discharge great quantities of Water. After pressing out the oil, the remainder is called cakes with which they heat ovens and burn them for fuel, they are exported to Holland where the cows are fed with them.

The machinery in these mills was, of course, identical to the horse mill described by Pyne. But still we have no indication of the construction of the windmills in which it was installed. The wind-powered cornmill was known in the Humber area from earliest times but there is no doubt that these early windmills would have been post mills. We must ask whether these early mills, which would have been comparatively light structures, would have been sufficiently substantial to carry the machinery used for oil seed crushing as described by the visitor to the Fens?

The arrangement described in 1696, installed in a post mill, would require extremely strong framing, as the single vertical runner stone would be constantly shifting the centre of gravity of the buck – unless of course, the mill was a hollow post mill, with the stones fixed at ground level. The hollow post mill was developed in Holland in the early part of the 15th century. It is generally accepted that it arrived in England in connection with land drainage schemes, although the precise date is not clear. Darby (*The Changing Fenlands*) states that the first intimation of an engine or mill being used for draining the Fens occurs in the 1570s. From 1575 onwards several proposals were put forward, culminating in Mostart's engine which we are fairly confident was a smock mill, the first of which was erected between 1597 and 1601. However, it does appear that a post mill was in use in the 1580s for land drainage purposes in the vicinity of Holbech which, in the light of present evidence, can only have been a hollow post mill.

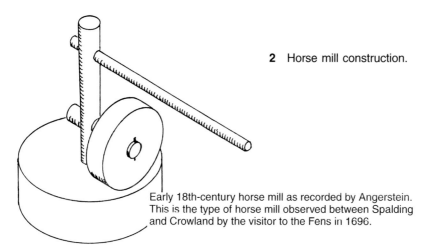

2 Horse mill construction.

Early 18th-century horse mill as recorded by Angerstein.
This is the type of horse mill observed between Spalding
and Crowland by the visitor to the Fens in 1696.

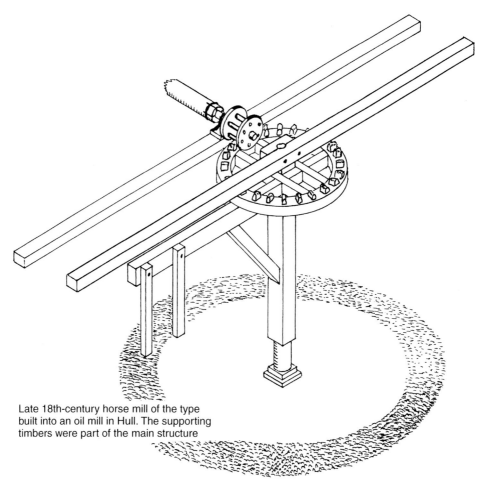

Late 18th-century horse mill of the type
built into an oil mill in Hull. The supporting
timbers were part of the main structure

We also know that in 1578 a wind-powered pump was built at Wollaton Colliery in Nottinghamshire, the construction of which will be considered in a later chapter.

Peter Filby has noted two post mills for crushing oil seed in Wisbech, one built during the 17th century, but by the mid-1600s the English post mill had become a reasonably strong structure (e.g. Bourn Mill in Cambridgeshire, built c.1626). Later still, a post mill at Melbourn (also in Cambridgeshire), built in the 18th century to grind corn, was at some stage converted to oil seed crushing.

It is recognised that there were post mills containing heavy oil milling machinery in Flanders, but these date from the late 18th century, by which time the post mill was a much more substantial structure than existed in England during the 14th century. There are other methods of crushing seed, using mechanical mortars and pestles: seed is placed in a pot and beaten from above by a pestle, operated from the windshaft by cams. An example exists at Villeneuve d'Ascq in northern France, but this also dates only from the 18th century and is again a very substantial structure. In the Russian North there are oil mills of a light build, where the pots (the mortars) are placed in a line down the centre of the mill and the windshaft (which carries cams to raise the pestle) is offset, an arrangement common in that area but so far unknown in England.

In the light of the above, there must be considerable doubt as to whether windmills were used for oil seed crushing before the introduction of the smock mill. It is most likely that the oil mill mentioned in Crowle (1381) was a horse mill and a similar conclusion might be drawn for the oil mill at Hull in 1525.

3   Diagram of a Russian oil mill.

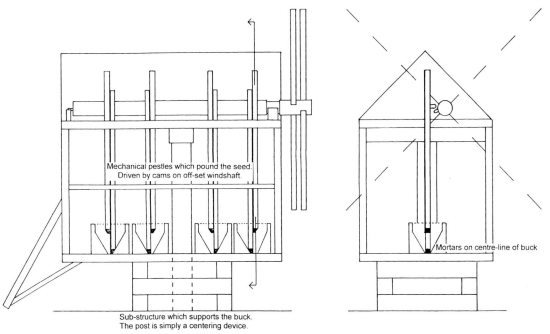

Mechanical pestles which pound the seed. Driven by cams on off-set windshaft.

Mortars on centre-line of buck

Sub-structure which supports the buck. The post is simply a centering device.

Against this latter point, there is a map of Hull which claims to show the town at the beginning of the 14th century and which includes a post mill approximately on a site which is known to have contained a wind-powered oil mill well into the 19th century. Consequently, this could point to the existence of a wind oil mill in the 14th century, which could possibly be the 1525 mill mentioned by Brace. We do not have any contemporary evidence to confirm this, so it cannot be more than a remote possibility.

By the date (1657) of the report of the traveller in the Isle of Axholme the smock mill had appeared in England, having been introduced at the end of the 16th century, as we have seen. It must be fairly certain that the Spalding mills were smock mills and at least likely that those on the Isle of Axholme were also, particularly as the latter were also in 'drained areas'. The smock mill is the design of the first wind-powered oil mill in England for which we have details of the structure, built at King's Lynn in 1638. Described as resembling a warehouse attached to a lofty windmill, the frame is claimed to have been brought over from Holland, and the depiction of the mill in a *Prospect of the Town* shows a typical Dutch smock mill.

Before this mill was erected, King's Lynn had experienced considerable difficulties over the application of mechanical power. The town's corn mill was water-powered but there had been a constant shortage of water. Several attempts had been made to redirect extra water to the mill from other streams but these attempts had not proved satisfactory. Consequently, during the 16th century the council authorised the erection of two wind-powered corn mills. The first was built in 1595 by John Ferne, a local millwright (for the sum of £35). For some reason this mill did not function satisfactorily and, after being moved to another site and then back to its original site, it was abandoned and eventually demolished in 1652. The second was never built. It is not surprising, therefore, that the oil merchant for whom the oil mill was built looked to the Dutch in preference to local millwrights.

The new oil mill was obviously successful, as a second oil mill was built in the town in 1680, again very typical of Dutch practice at that date, being a tall smock mill with wide braced stage, four common sails and winded by tailpole. The first mill was destroyed by fire in 1737 but the second was still in use in the 1740s and is thought to have survived for most of the 18th century.

The unfortunate paradox is that we do not have details of the plant installed in the King's Lynn mills. By that date the Dutch oil millers had developed an improved system for crushing seed which increased the extraction rate. The seed was first fed between cast-iron rollers to give it an initial bruising, the bruised seed then being placed under a pair of edge runner stones, to complete the crushing. (The action of these edge runner stones is sometimes misunderstood, the layout giving the impression that the seed was rolled. This is not the case; the very short radius on which the stones turn in fact produced a twisting action by the stones, perhaps a little similar to spinning a coin on a table top, the resultant action being a shearing effect on the seed.) The crushed seed was then placed on a heated

4 Millfleet Oil Mill, King's Lynn, built
in 1680 (based on a contemporary
engraving).

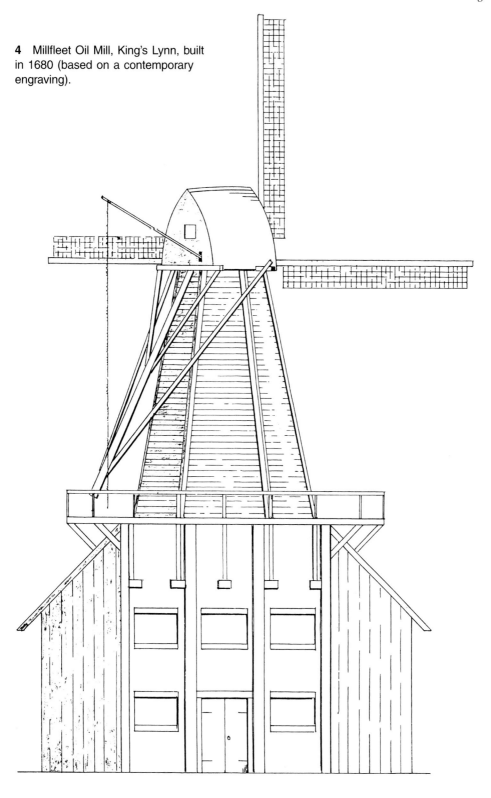

table, to reduce the viscosity of the oil, and then collected in small horse-hair bags ready for pressing, using the stamper press. These bags were placed in a trough, held upright by spacers, in-between which were placed two wedges, one apex downwards, one apex upwards. The first wedge was then hammered from above by a stout wooden stamper, which tightened the wedges and spacers, squeezing out the oil which ran into receptacles placed underneath the trough. When the operator judged all the oil had been pressed out, the first stamper was disconnected and a second stamper applied to the second wedge, which released the pressure. The iron rollers and edge runner stones, together with the cams that lifted the stampers, and a stirrer which agitated the seed on the heated table, were all driven by whatever power source was used – horse, wind or water.

It might be expected that the two Dutch oil mills built in King's Lynn would use the Dutch system of seed crushing but, in view of the description of the mills between Spalding and Crowland in 1696, some sixty years after the first mill was built in King's Lynn, it may well be that the simpler single-stone method was employed in the windmills at King's Lynn.

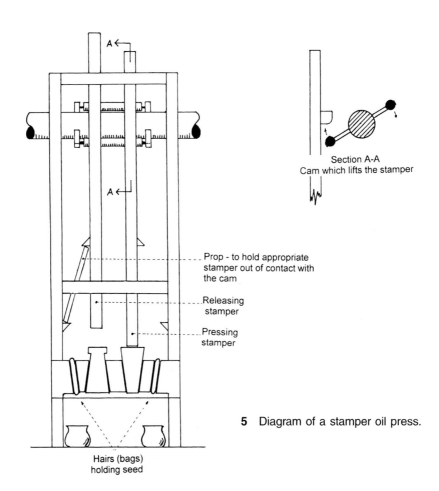

Section A-A
Cam which lifts the stamper

Prop - to hold appropriate stamper out of contact with the cam

Releasing stamper

Pressing stamper

5 Diagram of a stamper oil press.

Hairs (bags) holding seed

We must turn to Hull for the first clear indication of the use of the Dutch system. By 1700, several oil merchants were established in the town, in most cases using horse gins. But sometime before 1710 a small tower mill had been built in Church Street which certainly used the Dutch system. In 1719 it was damaged by fire and the remains were purchased by the leading oil miller, Joseph Pease, who repaired it and carried on crushing seed at the premises. Pease owned two other oil mills in the town, one a horse mill, while one shown on an engraving dated 1786 has all the appearance of a Dutch wip mill. There is evidence to suggest that this mill was in existence by 1735 and it certainly continued in use until 1800 when Pease consolidated his operations at the Church Street site.

By 1747 the small mill he had purchased and repaired in 1719 was proving inadequate and a letter from Pease to a business associate, Widow Morgan of Rotterdam, explains the position:

> You know my chief concern is in oil mills having 3 of my own one of which I purchased being a windmill about a quarter of a mile from this town [i.e. Church Street] near the river which I have had for about 28 years and at first pretty much

6 Salthouse Lane Oil Mill, Hull, built by 1735 and demolished in 1800. This mill has all the appearance of a Dutch wip mill.

altered the inside. The outside is not framed [i.e. built on a timber frame as a smock mill] but brick wall which the woodworks was before I bought it some years ago burnt. The mill is so low that from the ground one steps on the bars of the sails [this would indicate the height of the tower to be about 30/35ft to the curb]. The walls of it are not sufficient nor strong enough for raising the mill and the roof so bad that it is not worth repairing so must either stand still or must rebuild the same. I was inclined to rebuild in the same manner ... excepting having her about 20 foot higher and with a gallery and make all the in millwork do and serve again being very good most all being renewed in my time ... those in Holland with Pott Stamps and Presses is desirous and inclined to have it rebuilt in the best as with you [i.e. the Dutch] excepting brick walls. The mill has one pair of stones and but one press, one pair of iron rollers that flatten linseed and rapeseed before it is crushed under the stones. I desire you please to be so kind as to enquire after a sufficient sober and careful mill wright that complete and finish such a wind oil mill as good as any in Holland and on what terms he would come over here first to erect such mill ... also please inform me what such a small and true model of such a windmill would cost so as to serve as a pattern ... to execute and complete the mill before the end of November next. Please send me one of your best and latest printed mill books. I had one some time ago but parted with it to a friend at some distance from here.

Pease was a friend of John Smeaton, the leading engineer of the day, and one wonders if this is where Smeaton acquired one of his Dutch mill books.

The mill was duly built but the only plan we have of it shows a circular structure adjacent to a range of buildings, without any scale marked. However there is collateral information which enables us to draw up a reasonably clear picture. In 1754/5 John Smeaton designed a water-returning engine for this mill (which Pease decided not to go ahead with) and one of the drawings has a line marked 'Level of the windmill gallery floor', which, scaled off the drawing, is some 18ft 6ins above ground level. So we know the mill had a stage, a fact corroborated by a deed of adjoining property dated 1776 which includes a covenant to the effect that buildings on the site 'shall not go or be higher than the top of the mill gallery belonging to Joseph Pease'. Thus we can safely deduce that the mill was a tower mill, some 50/55ft to the curb, built of brick, with a wide braced stage, four common sails and winded by tailpole, very much the latest Dutch style. This view can be confirmed to some extent by a mill built further along Church Street in the 1780s for another oil miller, Joseph Moor, which is shown in a photograph of c.1894 to be very similar to the description of the Pease mill built around 1749.

So far as the internal plant of the Pease mill was concerned, we are more fortunate. Possibly as early as the 1750s Pease engaged Smeaton to replace the wooden poll end on the mill's windshaft with a cast-iron cross. No doubt to assess the strength of materials required, Smeaton drew a sketch of the internal machinery on which he noted the number of cogs on each gear wheel. The sketch shows the plant to be exactly that used by the Dutch as described above.

7 Tower of Moor's Oil Mill, Hull, built in 1781, as it stood *c*.1894.

By the 1750s, Smeaton was pioneering the use of cast iron in millwork, which he first applied to a wind-powered oil mill which he designed and built at Wakefield in 1755. The mill is described on Smeaton's drawing as an oil mill but it may have been built specifically for the manufacture of paint, as Smeaton also designed a 'rasper' and 'chipper' to produce dyes from the exotic hard woods being imported from South America and elsewhere. Generally it followed Dutch practice, the seed crushing plant (which was identical to that in the new Pease mill and which Smeaton may well have seen by this date) being contained in a rectangular brick building, above which extended a timber smock to carry the cap and four sails. The cap was not winded by a tailpole but by a continuous chain and pinion acting on a cogged ring inside the curb. This method of winding was known in Holland and may have already been in use in England, particularly in Lancashire and Anglesey. The innovative feature was the use of cast iron for the windshaft and the cast-iron cross at its outer end to which the sails were attached (which Stephen Buckland suggests may have been cast at Coalbrookdale).

John Smeaton's entry into the business of designing windmills was of considerable significance and the period around 1750 was a pivotal point for English windmill-building. In 1752 he decided to investigate the best design and layout for windmill sails. His experiments generally confirmed existing empirically derived practice, but he did conclude that the system which produced the 'best effect' was to have five sails. He was familiar with Dutch books containing windmill designs and in 1755 he went on a five-week tour of Flanders and the Low Countries, looking particularly at land drainage schemes and windmills. (He had already

8 Drawing of the internal layout of Pease's Oil Mill, Hull, built 1749-50. The numbers in the drawing indicate the number of cogs on each gear wheel. (Based on a sketch made by John Smeaton.)

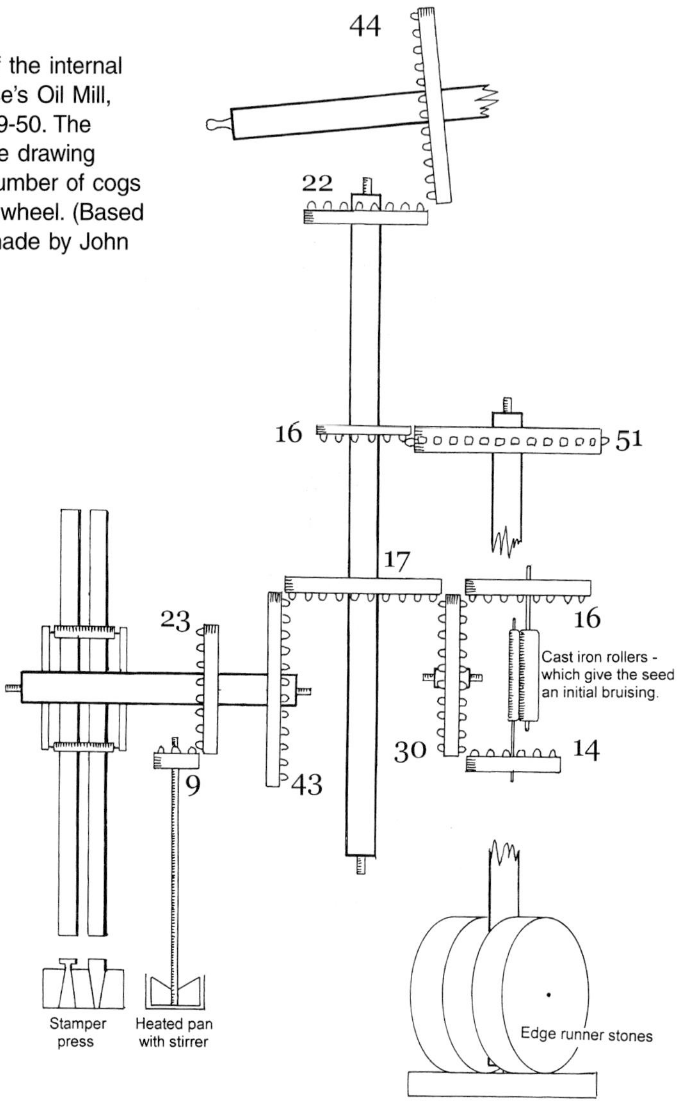

44

22

16   51

17

23

16

Cast iron rollers - which give the seed an initial bruising.

30   14

9   43

Stamper press   Heated pan with stirrer

Edge runner stones

completed the design for the Wakefield mill before he set off.) For his return journey, he boarded a ship at Schiedam, where he cannot have failed to notice the tall brick-built windmills around the town, very similar to the Pease oil mill erected in Hull.

The availability of cast iron was critical as it enabled Smeaton to implement his five-sail plan, which he first used in Leeds on a flint mill built in 1774. He designed a further oil mill in Leeds, for his son-in-law (there are no extant designs for this mill, although there is evidence to suggest it was a tower mill, and we can assume that he used his latest ideas) and finally a flour mill at Newcastle upon Tyne in 1782. These three mills had another new feature which depended for its success upon the availability of cast iron, the fan tail, which was to become the

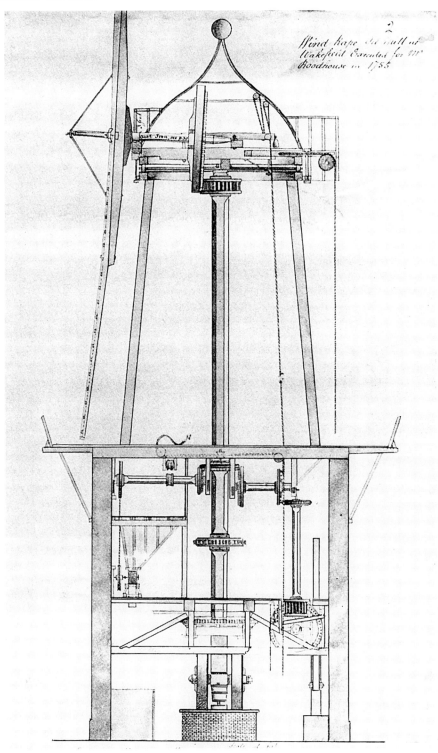

9 Smeaton's drawing for the oil mill at Wakefield built in 1754.

standard method of winding windmills in England. (The evolution of the fantail is considered in the chapter on materials for pottery and brick making.)

Up to this point windmills had been fitted with common sails but, during the second half of the 18th century, other improvements to sail design were to appear. The first to achieve any degree of success was put forward by the Scottish millwright, Andrew Meikle, who proposed what is now generally referred to as the spring sail. This sail comprised a number of hinged shutters (in appearance similar to a venetian blind) either of wood or canvas on a wire frame, which were fixed into the frame of the sail. Each shutter had a crank which was attached to a bar running the length of the main timber of the sail. Thus a longitudinal movement of the bar would open or close the shutters simultaneously. Having decided on the correct position (e.g. fully closed, half closed, etc.) in relation to the strength of the wind, the miller was able to fix the bar in the required position with a lever, held in place by a spring. If the wind speed increased the shutters would open slightly against the spring to spill the extra wind pressure. The sails still had to be set individually but their merit was that they introduced a degree of self-regulation. Meikle sent a plan of this arrangement to Smeaton in 1772 but rather surprisingly it does not seem to have been taken up until some later date and the idea was never patented.

The next improvement appeared in 1789 when Captain Stephen Hooper of Margate patented the roller reefing sail (Patent No 1706, 29 October 1789). A number of small roller blinds were substituted for the shutters of the spring sail, which were attached by webbing straps (called listings) to two longitudinal bars, one each side of the sail. Thus when the bars were moved longitudinally the roller blinds opened or closed, altering the effective sail area to varying degrees. However, unlike the spring sail, Hooper's longitudinal bars were connected to a central spider mounted on a rod (the striking rod) which passed through a hole bored down the centre of the windshaft. At the rear it was attached by either a bell crank with an extended arm, or in some cases a rack and pinion, to a looped chain which hung at the back of the mill, down to ground or stage level if one were provided. By pulling on the chain it was possible to adjust the sails, all at the same time and whilst the mill was still in motion. This was a positive step forward for the mill operator, the only drawback being that it was not self-regulating. This problem was overcome by adding boards along the leading edge of the sail which could turn through 90 degrees, controlled by a governor. In normal working the boards would be in line with the sail, but when activated by the governor (if the wind speed increased) they would turn at right angles, so breaking up the air flow and slowing down the sail.

Hooper's sail was tried out on two corn mills in Deal and was an immediate success. However, surprisingly, the main users of the patent were a firm of millwrights in Hull, Messrs Norman and Smithson. By 1791 they had become licensees for the patent, in which year the sails were applied to an oil mill built by the firm at Stoneferry in Hull. This mill was very much state of the art, being a tall tower mill with a braced stage and the five-sail plan recommended by Smeaton.

10 Windmills at Stoneferry, Hull. The mill on the left was an oil mill, built by Norman and Smithson in 1791; that on the right was a whiting mill, built a few years earlier. The fantails would have been in the form shown in the picture at a later date. Detail from a painting by John Ward, c.1830.

The design proved very satisfactory and in 1794 Norman and Smithson were engaged to build a new oil mill at Scawby, across the Humber in Lincolnshire. Of very similar design, the tower was eight storeys high, had a wide braced stage and five, probably roller, sails. Two oil mills also stood at West Ferry, along the River Trent, although the building date is not clear. They were certainly in existence by 1799 and may date from this period. Further along the Trent, two tall five-sail tower mills, very similar to the Hull and Scawby mills, were erected in 1802 and 1826 at Gainsborough, a town which had a wind-powered oil mill as early as 1709.

Moving back to East Anglia, a tall tower mill built at Cambridge in 1792 was converted to oil seed crushing in the 1820s but was demolished in 1845 following storm damage. In fact East Anglia seems to have followed the King's Lynn examples, a smock mill being built at Wisbech in 1771, which was used to crush oil seed until 1785, and another at Ramsey.

Smock mills were also used in Essex. An early example existed at West Ham, where Abbey Mills, a watermill built before 1679, later had a series of windmills built on the wharf, the windmill standing between 1703 and 1726 being used to produce rape and linseed oil. At Leyton, a windmill built by 1770 was noted as an oil mill in 1777. However, away from the marshes, a water-powered oil mill occurred at Wakes Colne, also in 1777.

Whilst the larger oil mills were using wind power during the 18th century, steam power had been tried in Hull, the first attempt being something of a disaster. At the beginning of the century, the town's water supply was obtained from the waterhouse in the centre of the town, which comprised a cistern on top of a tower into which the water was raised by a horse-powered pump. By 1773 the supply was inadequate and the Corporation decided to lease the waterhouse to Mayson Wright, an oil merchant, on condition that the lessee erected a steam engine to replace the horse gin. The engine was to work for six hours per day except Sundays, but the lessee was allowed to use as much of the premises as were not needed for the engine for his own purposes. He therefore installed an oil mill – an early example of off-peak energy.

Wright proposed to drive his oil mill using a water-returning engine, which he commissioned Smeaton to design. Smeaton's scheme proposed a 27ft-diameter water wheel to be fed from the cistern, with the water being raised, and returned, to the cistern by the steam-powered pump. Smeaton recommended Wright to use a Boulton & Watt engine but instead Wright decided to obtain one from Hindley of York. The engine was of an eclectic design, failed to work properly and eventually had to be replaced as Smeaton originally proposed.

After this unhappy experience there was a natural reluctance among Hull oil merchants to use steam. But when Boulton & Watt perfected their rotary engine in the 1780s, a firm of oil producers, Messrs Coates and Jarratt, who at that time were still relying on a horse gin to drive their oil mill, decided in 1784 to replace the gin with a Boulton & Watt steam engine (rated at 7hp). Their lead was followed by C. & J. Moorhouse of Gainsborough who installed a Boulton & Watt engine in 1787 (rated at 8hp) and by an oil miller in Walthamstow in 1789 and one in Spalding in 1790 (both rated at 4hp). In Hull, Joseph Pease's son in partnership with John Brooke (Smeaton's son-in-law) built a new oil mill in 1795 powered by a Boulton & Watt engine (rated at 16hp) and a year later a further engine was added to the Church Street site (rated at 12hp). But in spite of this foray into steam power, as late as 1810 a new wind-powered oil mill was built in the town for the Maister family, to replace their post mill, and in 1831 the editor of *White's Directory* was able to write, 'There are in Hull many extensive mills for grinding corn, paint colours and bones, for extracting oil from linseed, rape and other seeds: and for sawing timber and veneers. Most of them are set in motion by wind, some by steam.'

As late as 1827, a tall tower mill on Anlaby Road in Hull, built as a corn mill in the early part of the century, was converted to an oil mill specialising in the crushing of linseed. It was still in operation in 1876 but it is not certain that it

11 Maister Oil Mill, Hull, built to replace a post mill *c.*1810. Engraving by W.J. Cooke from a drawing by N. Whittock, 1829.

was still powered by wind at this date. One can only speculate as to why Hull merchants were reluctant to use steam power; one reason must be that the local millwrights were able to build windmills which could provide all the power needed by them at that date, and at an economic cost.

As we have seen, the early seed growing industry was located in the marshy areas around the Humber estuary, the Fens and the Essex Marshes, and the oil mills were sited near the source of the raw material. But during the 18th century, as more and more imported seed was used, oil mills started to appear at other ports. Three oil mills were erected in Liverpool: the first, a small tower mill certainly in operation in 1723 and possibly built as early as 1705, stood on the Mount, where the anglican cathedral stands today, but was demolished *c.*1805. A second mill appeared later in the century and in 1832 a mill in Oil Street was occupied by Earle & Carter, oil merchants. This latter mill was destroyed in a storm in 1839. In Newcastle upon Tyne an oil mill at Stepney, built as a four-sail brick tower mill (possibly in 1779), was remodelled by Smeaton in 1783 when he added a new cast-iron windshaft and five sails. A drawing of the mill made in 1838 shows it with a horizontal fantail which was most likely constructed when the mill was first built. The internal plant comprised the standard edge runner stones and stamper press. Wind power was still in use in 1858 and the mill may well have continued into the 1880s. Louis Simonds in 1811 recorded innumerable windmills in the area around Alnwick, being used for both grain milling and crushing oil seed. He describes them in sufficient detail for us to establish that these mills had fantails and that the sails were self-reefing. Although Cubitt's patent sail had appeared by this date, 1811 must surely be very early for the patent to have reached Northumberland, so it is possible they were Hooper's roller sails, which in turn may show a connection with the Hull area. (The phraseology used by Simond precludes the option of spring sails.)

12 Stepney Oil Mill, Newcastle upon Tyne, built in 1783. The five-sail arrangement was designed by John Smeaton. Detail from an engraving from a drawing by J.W. Carmichael, 1838.

Further south, at Stakesby on the Yorkshire coast, a three-storey tower mill built as a corn mill in 1778 was used for a few years for crushing oil seed. And at Stockton on Tees a small wooden smock mill, with a cast-iron windshaft, was built in 1790 as a combined corn and oil mill, although by 1794 it was being used solely as a corn mill. Brace mentions oil mills near Warwick on the River Avon (1704) and Evesham (1730), which were probably watermills and would presumably have obtained imported seed by barge via the River Avon.

There were also a few isolated oil mills. At Devizes, a pair of tower mills built as early as 1713 (to produce oil for the lamps of the nearby City of Bath?) were only short-lived, lasting until 1740 when they were converted to snuff milling. At Hawkstone Park, in Shropshire, a mill was built c.1795 to crush linseed grown on the estate to produce cattle feed. But in addition to this fundamentally practical use, the mill also had a secondary function. Hawkstone Park was the country seat of the Hill family, who achieved fame in a variety of ways, one being the 'improvement' of the natural features in the Park, to produce intricate pathways, ravines, arches, bridges and towering cliffs, embellished with a number of follies, e.g. a hermitage complete with a live hermit, grottos, caves and a number of buildings. One such building, a cottage known as Neptune's Whim, was described in the 1799 guide book issued to visitors, as follows: 'This whimsical edifice is built in the exact taste of the houses in North Holland (with a windmill on the opposite bank of the river, painted quite in the Dutch Style) ...'

Thus the windmill also served as a folly in the Park's 'picturesque' landscape. But whatever its external appearance, it was nevertheless a practical working oil mill (at a later date it was also used to crush bone for use as fertiliser). The mill was a brick tower, battered, and had a wide braced stage at first-floor level, which would give a Dutch appearance. It had a cap typical of the area with four common sales mounted on a cast-iron windshaft, but the Dutch tail pole was rejected in favour of the more practical English winding wheel and chain. It is understood that the millwright was William Hazeldine. Hawkstone mill is the only surviving example of an English wind-powered oil mill. It still has its windshaft in place together with the upright shaft and some gearing. A modern cap has been fixed which will protect the internal remains from the weather, until such time as a more complete restoration can be carried out.

On the subject of oil milling, reference must be made to an unusual mill which was built at Battersea in 1788, to the design of Captain Hooper, for a maltster named Hodgson. The design comprised an horizontal windmill, with the sails turning on a vertical axis erected in an octagonal wooden tower, the sides of which were fitted with slats which could be opened or closed to control the flow of wind onto the sails. This form of construction dates back to the ninth century and is the earliest known practical form of windmill. The idea was taken up in China where it was used to pump water and R. D'acres, writing in 1659, gives a clear indication that horizontal wind engines were known in

13 Hawkstone Park Oil Mill, built *c*.1795 as part of the Hawkstone Follies. This was, nevertheless, a functional oil mill.

England at that date, although it was recognised that they were not as powerful as wind engines with vertical sails. Nevertheless, the concept had tempted engineers from time to time and perhaps inevitably, in an age of mechanical innovation, several industrial windmills with horizontal sails were attempted. The best known examples are those designed by Hooper at Margate, Battersea and Sheerness. The Battersea mill was used to crush linseed but after only four years it was converted to corn milling. It eventually fell into disrepair and was finally demolished in 1849 when Battersea Park was laid out. This form of construction was never a success, as horizontal mills were susceptible to storm damage and expensive to maintain. Nevertheless, in an age of scientific experiment and discovery, one can imagine the active mind speculating on such ideas.

Finally, Rex Wailes gives the names of five wind-powered oil mills in Kent, at Challock Lees, Eastry, Gillingham, West Farleigh and Wormshill. Coles-Finch (*Watermills and Windmills*) gives details of mills in these locations but when he visited them they were all in use as corn mills. He does, however, mention that Huggin's Mill in Gillingham had been built as an oil-cake mill and later converted to corn, but gives no dates. Brace notes that oil millers were shown in the directories of 1847 and 1849 at Wormshill and at Tutsham Mill, West Farleigh up to 1889, when it was burnt down. Interestingly, Brace also notes that John Rennie is reputed to have designed this mill in 1808. Mills in these locations were probably used at some time during their life to produce oil cake, possibly for local agricultural use.

As has been mentioned, the expansion of oil milling into new locations resulted in the use of water power, and, in a few places where water power was available, it was also used in the established oil milling locations. A particular example is a small area to the south of Cambridge where a dozen or so watermills were either built or converted to oil production specifically to meet the need for lamp oil for the metropolis. Unfortunately, at about the same time gas lighting began to appear in the public streets and this market faded away. Nevertheless, it was in the established industry location, using wind power that the industry thrived, in particular on the Humber estuary and its serving rivers, e.g. at Hull, Gainsborough, Selby.

During the 19th and 20th centuries Hull became the major site for oil seed crushing in England; of the one hundred and fifty or so presses at work in 1856, about one hundred were operating in Hull. In addition to providing direct employment, the presence of the oil mills in the town resulted in the development of other industries, in particular paint making and specialist engineering firms to fabricate and develop seed crushing machinery. To emphasise the extent of Hull's domination, we can look at the list of all seed merchants shown in trade directories, compiled by Brace:

Town	Number of seed crushers listed
Hull	266
London	71
Liverpool	47
Leeds	26
Gainsborough	22

It must be emphasised that in no case were the firms listed in each town in business at the same time: there were never 266 mills in Hull at any one moment and some of the firms listed only existed for a few years. But it does show where merchants were trying to establish their businesses.

Having said that, during the 19th century the industry was not solely confined to the ports listed above. Brace lists a further 143 firms spread across 88 different towns, mainly on the eastern side of England, from Kent to East Yorkshire. The towns in this subsidiary group with the largest number of merchants were King's Lynn with eight, Grimsby and Norwich with six each, after which it is quite clear that many market towns had their own oil mill, probably producing cake for use by local farmers and oil for local lighting purposes. Most of these firms appear from about 1820 onwards and, whereas several used wind or water power, the majority would have used the small steam engines which were becoming available.

In the 200 years from 1638 when the oil mill in King's Lynn was built, some 37 wind-powered oil mills were built in England, several of which continued to operate well into the 19th century. But by 1800, six of the new Boulton & Watt engines had been introduced into the industry and, during the 19th century, as the oil milling concerns grew larger and the steam engine became more economic, wind power gave way to steam.

3

Crushing Materials
for Pottery Manufacture

For centuries, man has produced pots from whatever local clay he could find for use as storage vessels. But when, during the 17th century, Western Europe was introduced to the pleasures of drinking tea and coffee, an immediate demand arose for a suitable drinking vessel. This demand was met initially by the import of delicate white porcelain from the Far East. Inevitably European potters tried to produce similar wares, the first to succeed being the Meissen factory near Dresden. In England the first potters to copy Chinese porcelain were located in Bristol, Liverpool and London, the ports where the original ware had first been seen.

To achieve this end, potters experimented with a variety of materials for the body of the pot and its decoration, all of which involved crushing and mixing the basic ingredients. Traditionally this had been done by hand, or in some cases by horse mill, but, as demand increased, potters looked to the traditional sources of mechanical power, i.e. water wheels and windmills. One of the new materials used by potters in the manufacture of porcelain was flint and this material in particular required considerable power to crush the calcined nodules into powder form.

Two early attempts to produce 'china' occurred at the well known factories established in London during the 1740s, at Bow (1748-76) and Chelsea (1744-84). It has been suggested that a watercolour, painted by H. O'Neale in the 1760s, shows the Bow Factory with three post mills nearby which may have been used to grind materials. This is quite definitely not the case. The building in the picture is not Bow Pottery and the windmills, which are noted by Kenneth Farries (*Essex Windmills, Millers and Millwrights*), were used solely as corn mills. Similarly there are sketches of a smock mill which stood on the banks of the Thames and which, it has been suggested, may have been used to produce glazes from lead oxide for the nearby Chelsea factory, but there is no evidence to link this mill to the pottery other than proximity.

Much clearer is the case of another windmill which attracted the attention of artists (e.g. John Varley, two of whose paintings of this mill were included in the exhibition mentioned in the first chapter). It stood on the south bank of the Thames at Nine Elms, Vauxhall and appears to have been in existence by the mid-1750s, at which date John Smeaton was involved. He designed a set of sails together with a set of crushing tubs and related gearing. What is not clear is whether this was a new mill at that date or, as seems more likely, he carried out

14 Randall's China Mill at Nine Elms, Vauxhall, built mid-1750s. Watercolour by John Varley 1830.

improvements to one already in existence. The sails were common sails but with the outer end splayed, as he recommended following his experiments in 1751 and 1752, and winding was by winding wheel and chain, as he used on his oil mill at Wakefield. The crushing tubs, eight in all, spaced round the upright shaft, had stone nuts larger in diameter than the spur wheel. Consequently, to enable the stone nuts to engage the spur wheel, the latter would have been a deep lantern pinion, with the stone nuts engaging alternately higher and lower. In the mid-1820s, the power unit was modernised, the common sails being replaced by patent sails and a fantail added.

The mill was clearly used for the preparation of materials for the manufacture of china, and the watercolours by John Varley, painted around 1830, show two kilns, which may have been used for calcining flint or, more likely at that date, animal bone. The mill would have supplied premises in Vauxhall and, possibly, in the mill's early days, the Chelsea factory across the river.

An important requirement by the potters was a readily available source of coal to fire the kilns. This was well met in the North Staffordshire area, where the main developments in the English ceramic industry occurred. At the beginning of the 18th century, the area was still very rural but many smallholders took advantage of the clay to be found amongst local coal seams to produce pots in their spare time. Typical wares were butter pots, milk pans and storage vessels. These items lacked the quality of the fine imported porcelain, but there was an undoubted body of expertise and skill in the area which formed a solid base on which the new industry could be built.

The 1720s was the period during which new developments came to the fore. Thomas Astbury started to experiment with the use of crushed flint and clays other than those locally available. His lead was followed and developed by others, in particular by various members of the Wedgwood family.

A critical factor, as in any manufacturing process, was the preparation of the raw materials. Clay was comparatively easy to crush and mix with water but flint was a more difficult proposition. Early attempts were made to crush flint with stampers, the established practice in metal mines, and with ordinary millstones. Neither was satisfactory; the millstones suffered severe damage but, more importantly, the fine dust which was created by both methods was fatal to the operator's lungs. In 1726 Thomas Benson, a local engineer, patented a system of grinding flint in water which involved using large iron balls. This proved unacceptable as iron from the balls became intermixed with the flint, which, when added to the clay, produced staining. In 1732 Benson replaced the iron balls with ones made of stone.

Benson's patent stated that his machine was to be driven by a water wheel. There is uncertainty as to where and when the first water-powered flint mill was built. Simeon Shaw (*History of the Staffordshire Potteries*) writes that the first mill for this purpose 'was erected at Cookshut Green, about two miles from Bemersley [i.e. to the NE of Tunstall] afterwards a second at the Meir near Furnace [i.e. Longton] and another at Ivy House in Hanley'. But he later writes that 'the first attempt at grinding flint in a slop or wet state, was at Ivy House, by a small waterwheel'. No dates are given but the more recent RCHME publication (*Potworks*) states that 'a number of watermills were adapted from corn mills, e.g. Gomm's Mill, bought by John Peate in Lane Delph, in 1732, the old machine mill at Little Chell, used for potting from 1746. Around this date Thomas Whielden was operating his own watermill at Fenton.'

From reference to contemporary maps, it seems likely that Gomm's mill, converted in 1732, is the one referred to by Shaw at Furnace, and the mill at Little Chell, converted in 1746, was that referred to at Cookshut Green. These mills are respectively at the north and south ends of the area known as the Six Towns. Barry Job (*Watermills of the Moddershall Valley*) has looked at this in some detail and concluded that Ivy House was the first wet grinding mill. It is reasonable to assume from the above that this mill was built shortly after the first patent was taken out by Benson, i.e. in the late 1720s. These three mills were owned by John Gallimore and the builder, or millwright, was Joseph Bourne. The mills used Benson's basic concept but incorporated 'very important improvements suggested by James Brindley'.

It is not clear at what stage Brindley became involved with mills in the potteries. Shortly after completing his apprenticeship as a millwright in 1740, he set up in business in Leek, but by 1750 he had decided to move to Burslem, where he rented a workshop from Thomas and John Wedgwood. At that date

Burslem was one of the villages which later became known as the Six Towns. The village was described as

> ... a broad straggle of houses [which] runs along the top of the hill, with the church in the valley below. The shops of a cobbler, a barber and a couple of butchers are dotted amid clusters of potworks and inns ... . Between the potteries lie triangles of common land and lanes twisting outwards to meadows and crofts. ... the landscape was ... gouged with pots and humped mounds of drying clay and towering shard rucks of spoiled pots. And on every side great bottle-shaped kilns curved and smoked against the sky.

Brindley probably moved to Burslem in anticipation of good opportunities for employment, anticipation which could have arisen from his involvement in some of the early attempts to grind flint using water power. We know for certain that in 1757 he built a water-powered flint mill at Moddershall to the south of the Six Towns.

15 Tower of Burslem Flint Mill as it stood *c.*1850, built by James Brindley in 1750.

One of the prime difficulties facing the emerging potteries in mid-century was poor communications between the sources of raw materials and their markets. The new materials used in the search for white wares – china clay and flint – were unavailable in Staffordshire, they were imported from Devon, Cornwall and the shores of South East England, respectively, which inevitably involved heavy transport costs. Materials were brought as close as possible by sea and inland waterway, but the last part of the journey was by packhorse. Even after the turnpiking of roads in the 1760s, transport costs were still high, as many mills were several miles from the early factories and road tolls had to be paid twice, once to transport flint to the mill and a second time on the return journey. Being sited 'along the top of the hill', and thus some distance from the sites of the mills so far mentioned, Burslem's many potters were in a worse position than most.

These problems brought Brindley two interesting commissions. Shortly after settling in Burslem he met the need for a flint mill in the village by erecting a wind-powered flint crushing mill. The mill comprised a three-storey cylindrical tower, probably no more than 30ft to the curb, fitted with four common sails.

The design of the cap and method of winding are not known. Eliza Meteyard (*The Life and Works of Wedgwood*) describes this mill as 'of greater power than any yet known in the district, for grinding calcined flints'. Unfortunately, on its first day in operation the sails blew off in a high wind. Undaunted, Brindley carried out repairs and the mill continued to work for many years. It seems to have been out of use by the time Simeon Shaw was published in 1829 but the empty tower was extant as late as 1865.

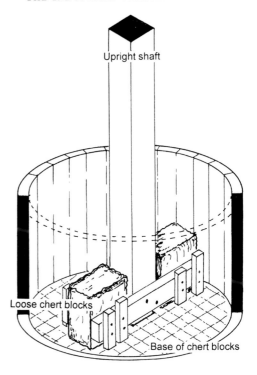

16 Diagram of an 18th-century flint crushing pan (based on sketch in John Rennie's diary).

The Burslem mill represents an important step in the evolution of the flint mill. Brindley installed a developed version of Benson's patent. His crushing tub was much larger in diameter than Benson envisaged, comprising a circular timber construction with the base made of blocks of chert (i.e., the same material which comprises flint). The upright shaft came directly down the mill tower with its footstep bearing in the centre of the tub. Arms were attached to the shaft which pushed round large blocks of chert as it rotated. Nineteenth-century versions had four arms made of cast iron but in the mill at Leeds Pottery, built twenty years later than Brindley's at Burslem, and where the arms were made of timber, there were only two arms. (Leeds Pottery will be mentioned shortly.) The nodules to be crushed were first calcined and then placed in the tub and the large blocks of chert were placed on top of them. As the sails turned, the arms at the lower end of the upright shaft pushed the large blocks of chert around inside the tub and the flint was crushed between the loose chert blocks and the fixed blocks forming the base. Thus was established the central feature of flint mills which remained in use for some 200 years. The water was supplied by a well from which it was raised by a pump driven from a crown wheel on the upright shaft.

One final point on the construction of Brindley's mill concerns the gear ratio between the brakewheel and the wallower. In the case of most corn tower mills this is usually around a 1:2 step-up in speed, the upright shaft turning at twice the speed of the windshaft. If this were the case at Burslem, assuming the sails turned at around 12 rpm, the arms in the crushing tub would be turning at something like 24rpm, which is most unlikely. If one considers the restored water-powered flint mill at Cheddleton, where all the gearing and shafts are of iron, the arms in the pan appear to be designed to turn at about 6rpm. Although the pan is probably larger in diameter than that at Brindley's windmill, using this as a guide, the ratio between the brakewheel and the wallower at Burslem would be the reverse of the norm, i.e. 2:1 step-down in speed. Interestingly, Meteyard describes the gearing as 'unusually large' which would be an apt description of an arrangement where the wallower was much larger than the brakewheel. Also, if this was the case and assuming the brake wheel was still fairly large, then the brakewheel would need to be located well forward on the windshaft, to accommodate the large wallower. It is likely, therefore, that the cap would be boat-shaped or simply a pent roof. It was unlikely to have been domed.

So, Brindley's first contribution to the potters of Burslem was to build them a mill which, apart from the general convenience of having one close at hand, would have helped to reduce their transport costs. The second interesting contribution arising from the transport problems was his acceptance of the commission to design the Trent and Mersey and the Calder canals, finally opened in 1777, which linked the Six Towns with the ports of Liverpool and Hull, giving a much better access to the markets of London and North America – and, of course, to the source of materials. Sir George Head (*A Home Tour through the Manufacturing Districts of England in 1835*) gives us an indication of the importance of the canal to the potteries, when, on his visit to the quays at Runcorn, he observed:

> The enormous heaps of material piled up, ready for embarkation, would be suf-
> ficient, one would think, to freight all the barges on the line for months to come;
> consisting of substances used in the manufacture of British China – such as flints
> from Kent and Sussex, pipe-clay from Devonshire and Dorsetshire, besides a
> soft stone containing an abundance of mica from Cornwall and Wales ... the
> enormous heaps of flint and materials, each neatly piled and labelled with the
> owner's name ...

By the 1760s the most entrepreneurial potters were employing increasingly large workforces, which resulted in the division of labour and employees spec- ialising in various stages of production (but still relying upon the manual skills of individual employees). This required new layouts for factories, individual rooms being provided for each process, which not only increased efficiency but also helped to safeguard newly invented processes. One of the leaders in this was Josiah Wedgwood, who in 1769 erected an entirely new factory on a greenfield site to the south of Burslem, with houses for his workforce, thus creating an embryonic new village which he called Etruria.

17 Wedgwood's Etruria Works and windmill built in 1779. Painting by Stebbing Shaw, 1794.

It is suggested that he initially continued to use Brindley's windmill some miles away at Burslem, but by 1774 he had erected a new windmill at the northern end of the new factory. A painting by Stebbing Shaw dated 1794 shows the mill as an extremely tall tower mill with a stage above the level of the adjoining buildings, fitted with six sails and an early type of horizontal fantail. It is likely that the fantail was added in the 1780s – Wedgwood had been in correspondence with Smeaton on the subject and in a letter dated 26 January 1782 Smeaton commented that the fantail was in common use on the windmills around Leeds. We also know that the Wedgwood accounts show a payment of £189 15s. 0d. in 1787 for expenditure on the windmill, a figure which would more than cover the cost of adding a fantail.

The windmill was initially used to grind clay bodies but it seems that the demand outstripped its capacity and, in 1782, Wedgwood took a lease of Fenton Watermill on the River Trent, a long established corn mill which was converted to flint grinding at about that date. The two mills were thereafter used in tandem for several years, the windmill being used for experimental work. Difficulties were experienced as in some cases a particular material ground at the windmill did not turn out the same when ground in larger quantities at the watermill.

The builder of the windmill is not recorded. It is interesting to note that Wedgwood had been presented with an alternative design by Erasmus Darwin, a fellow member of the Lunar Society. This is usually described as a horizontal mill but it was quite different in concept from the horizontal mill designed by Hooper and mentioned in the chapter on oil seed crushing. Darwin's mill comprised an octagonal wooden tower with the sides made of horizontal slats hinged at the bottom. The upright shaft had triangular sails attached horizontally at its top end. The theory was that the slats facing the wind would be opened to allow the wind to enter and it would then have no option but to flow upwards, passing the sails and causing them to turn. It is not clear how the slats were controlled but, if they were spring-mounted, they would be self-controlling, a nice feature. Again, one can imagine the active mind speculating on such ideas. When he built his first mill, Wedgwood obviously chose to follow the example of Brindley's Burslem mill, but in 1779 he was still seeking more power and the horizontal scheme was again under consideration. To his credit, Darwin was also advising Wedgwood to consider acquiring a Boulton & Watt steam engine, but at this stage Watt had not perfected his rotary motion. By 1782 the situation had improved and Wedgwood ordered his first steam engine from Boulton & Watt. The single surviving drawing indicates that the engine was to drive a roller crushing mill, a pair of two-foot diameter stones for grinding enamels, a reciprocating sieve and a single stamper of about sixty pounds weight. However the engine was not installed until 1784, by which time the stamper had been replaced by two cam-operated hammers and a nine-foot diameter pan had been added. The sieve may have been omitted.

Two matters should be mentioned here. First, some writers have claimed that Darwin's horizontal mill was actually built, but there is no evidence to support this view. Secondly, the claim has been made that the two entries relating to engines in the Boulton & Watt papers indicate that two engines were installed, in 1782 and 1784; again, the evidence does not support this view. Some ten years later Wedgwood installed a second Boulton & Watt engine and the windmill seems to have gone out of use shortly after that date.

One other potter, Enoch Wood, used wind power into the 1780s at his factory, which was also in Burslem, for 'raising water, mixing clay and grinding glazes

18 Enoch Wood's Pottery and windmill tower built at Burslem in 1750, as shown in a drawing c.1843.

and colours'. The description of the work done by the windmill is interesting as it clearly omits the grinding of flint. In fact, very few of the potteries undertook this part of the operation in the factory – they either leased a separate mill or purchased the flint from specialist producers. Most of these flint mills were water-powered, either converted from existing corn mills or purpose-built. In some cases Newcomen-type engines were used to increase the capacity of a watermill by pumping water from the tail race back over the water wheel, e.g. at Lane End and the Spode factory (both *c.*1775) and during the 19th century steam-powered flint mills were erected. Nevertheless, many water mills continued in operation until the 1950/60s, mainly along the Moddershall and Churnet Valleys. During the 20th century several of these mills also ground animal bone, much in demand for bone china.

By the second half of the 18th century, the windmill was obviously recognised by potters as a useful power source. Another example occurred at Leeds when a new pottery was built around 1770, possibly on the site of an earlier pottery. The mill comprised a tower of some 50 feet to the curb, probably having four sails. In 1774 the sails were blown off in a storm and were replaced by a set of five sails designed by John Smeaton, the first use of his preferred sail plan. It has been said that Smeaton was called in to design new sails following the collapse, but Stephen Buckland has pointed out that Smeaton had prepared his design before the disaster occurred. The mill had another important feature, a fantail, probably part of the original structure, which extended horizontally at the rear of the cap.

The fantail was the brainchild of Edmund Lee, a blacksmith working at Brock Forge, near Wigan, who patented the invention in 1745/6 (Patent No 615, 9 December 1745). Lee's fantail comprised a set of small sails at the rear of the mill, mounted on and geared to a wheel which ran on the ground, the whole fan assembly being mounted on the outer end of the tail pole. The principle was that, when the wind blew directly at the sails, it divided into two streams which passed either side of the mill body, and at the rear exerted equal pressure on either side of the fan; thus the fan remained static. If, however, the wind hit the main sails at an oblique angle, then one of the divided streams of air would exert more pressure on the fan than the other, causing the fan to turn and thus drive the wheel making it push the tail pole, and consequently turn the cap, until the point was reached where the two streams were again exerting an equal force on the fan. At this point the main sails would again be facing directly into wind. We know that two mills with this arrangement were built in the Wigan area around 1750, not by Lee but by a local engineer called Richard Melling. One was a corn mill and the other at a coal mine belonging to Sir Richard Brock, where it was used to drive pumps. How well this design achieved its purpose can only be guessed at; it is very doubtful whether the wheel in contact with the ground would have had sufficient purchase to work effectively.

Returning now to Leeds, the fantail on the mill at the pottery was not a simple copy of the Lee/Melling design but a much improved arrangement. Here, whoever built this mill put a cogged wheel on the curb (as Smeaton had done on the

Wakefield oil mill) but, instead of the winding wheel and chain, he had constructed a frame which extended horizontally to the rear of the cap, on which he mounted a fan. The fan was connected by gears and shafting to a pinion which meshed with the cogged ring on the curb, an arrangement which would overcome any problems of the wheel slipping. Thus it appears that some unrecorded engineer or millwright, working in Leeds and probably having some knowledge of the Wigan mills, saw the benefit of combining the winding wheel and the Lee/Melling fan to produce the first practical fantail for a tower mill. This self-winding device was a major step forward in mill design, relieving the mill operator of the need to monitor the wind direction and turn the sails manually into wind.

There is no indication of who the engineer may have been. It seems unlikely to have been Smeaton, but from about 1760 the Leeds to Liverpool Canal (which passes through Wigan) was being surveyed and from 1770 was under construction, so plenty of people of a mechanical bent were passing between Wigan and Leeds. Indeed, in the 1760s James Brindley was engaged to review the proposal and the resident engineer for the canal was a former pupil of Smeaton's.

In the early years, the flints for use by the Leeds potters were brought by sea from Kent and Sussex to Hull and Selby, where they were transferred to barges to continue the journey to Leeds via the Aire and Calder Navigation. Kidson (*The Leeds Pottery*) states that at some date a dispute arose over freight costs, so the firm transferred its flint-grinding operation to a rented watermill at Thorpe Arch near Wetherby, which, even though the last five miles of the journey was by road, proved beneficial to the proprietors of the pottery. One writer has suggested

19 Leeds Pottery Mill, built *c.*1770. The sails were designed by John Smeaton and added in 1774. This mill had the first confirmed application of the horizontal fantail, although there may have been other contemporary examples in Leeds. From a bill head.

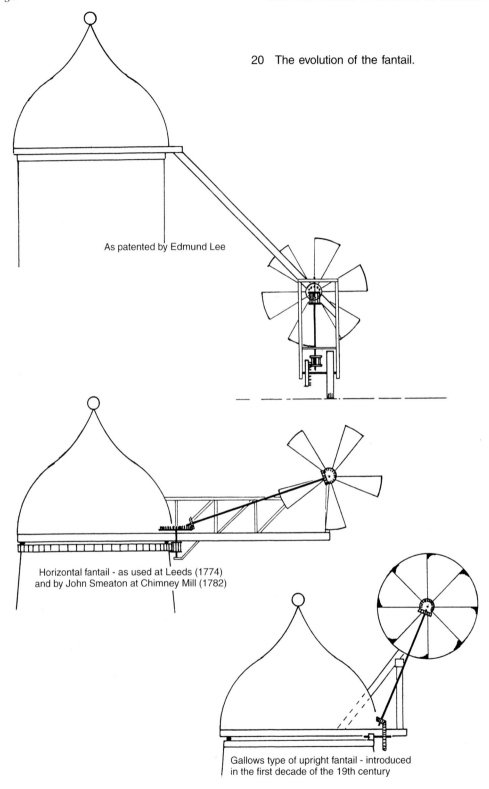

20   The evolution of the fantail.

As patented by Edmund Lee

Horizontal fantail - as used at Leeds (1774)
and by John Smeaton at Chimney Mill (1782)

Gallows type of upright fantail - introduced
in the first decade of the 19th century

that the move occurred in 1775 and that thereafter the windmill was taken out of use. This was not the case. In 1784, John Rennie undertook a tour of Northern England, recording his observations in his diary. On 5 January 1784 he was in Leeds and visited this mill, which was in production at the time, and described its internal machinery.

Starting with the top (fourth) floor, he explained that there was a tub for grinding black colours, constructed 'exactly like a tub for grinding of flint' which had two stones (i.e., blocks not millstones) carried round by an arm on each side of the axis. On the third floor were five tanks, one larger than the others. The large one was 4ft 4ins diameter and 4ft 6ins deep, and contained stones similar to that on the top floor. The smaller ones, driven by belts from the upright shaft, were of various sizes – 3ft 8ins x 1ft 4ins; 1ft 4ins x 1ft 4ins; 1ft 6ins x 1ft 8ins and 2ft 8ins x 2ft 6ins. They were described as 'a little tapered' and a horizontal stone was suspended from a shaft which revolved close to the bottom of the tub. They were used to grind colours and from the description seem very much like tubs used to crush paint dyes at that date. On the second floor were two flint crushing tubs, both 7ft diameter and 3ft 6ins deep. On the first floor was a wash tub into which the slop would flow from the flint pans on the floor above. From here the slop passed along a pipe or channel through the wall into the factory. On the ground floor was a pair of edge runner stones, 5ft 6ins diameter and 1ft thick, with metal tyres, turning on a 6ft stone bed. These were used to crush material for making moulds, probably gypsum. Although not mentioned by Rennie, one might have expected the mill to contain a pump and some form of hoist. By any standards this was an impressive structure.

As is noted above, early attempts to produce pottery to match wares being imported from Europe took place at the original ports of entry. One such was Liverpool, where several porcelain factories existed during the second half of the 18th century. One of these factories, the Herculaneum Pottery (1796-1840), was located on the bank of the River Mersey some two or three miles to the south of the town centre. In 1806 the company included a picture of the factory on its share certificate which shows a number of bottle kilns and a windmill at each end of the site. The form of construction is somewhat unusual as they were both open trestle post mills, without any cladding on the buck. The trestle is in each case mounted on a rectangular structure which, it has been suggested, contained water tanks, and that the mills were hollow post mills for pumping water from wells on site. This seems a likely conclusion, but the possibility that the mills provided power for some part of the factory cannot be ruled out. The windmills at the Herculaneum Pottery continued in use until replaced by a steam engine in 1818.

Another thriving port by the end of the 17th century, although probably not importing china, was Whitehaven, on the coast of Cumbria. In 1699 an expert from the Staffordshire potteries was invited to advise on the suitability of local clays for pottery manufacture. His report was encouraging and shortly afterwards production commenced. At first the wares were limited to clay pipes but in 1813

21 Two windmills at Herculaneum Pottery, Liverpool, built in 1796, as shown on the company's share certificate.

and 1819 a new pot works opened producing a full range of household articles. One of the new pot works included a windmill to power machinery for grinding and mixing clay.

Finally, a windmill on the other side of the Pennines, at Stockton on Tees, was used for a short period in connection with a pottery. A large brick tower mill, built in 1786 and thought to be the first of the tower mills on the Tees estuary, was fitted up to grind corn and crush oil seed. The oil crushing machinery would probably have been located on the ground floor and the corn milling machinery above, as in the case of the still-surviving mill at Deerlijk in Holland. The Stockton mill seems to have operated simply as a corn mill from 1794 but it is recorded that in the late 19th century the mill was providing power to puddle clay for use at the Clarence Pottery.

4

Crushing Materials for Use in the Manufacture of Paint

Paint was much in demand to protect and decorate the many new iron structures which began to appear at the end of the 18th century. As we have seen, oil produced from seed was a basic ingredient of paint, linseed being the preferred choice. Lead was the second ingredient, white lead (lead carbonate) being used as a base due to its combined opacity, covering power and quick drying characteristics. To this base of oil and white lead a pigment or mixture of pigments would be added to produce the desired colour. Red lead (lead oxide), produced by roasting white lead, was one such pigment. Whether used as a base or a pigment, the material had to be crushed.

Lead was also used by potters as a glaze. Farries and Mason suggest that a smock mill near the Chelsea Pottery might have been used for this purpose but this must be doubtful, as Angerstein makes no mention of it in his notes of a visit to the factory in 1750. With more certainty, Gareth Hughes records that a windmill was used to grind glazes at one of the four potteries in Prescott, a few miles from Liverpool. It is known to have been in existence by 1814 and was still extant in 1848. No details of its construction have survived but Hughes notes that there is evidence that the mill was probably a very slim tower mill, only some five feet in diameter at the base. This must indicate that the mill drove machinery in an adjoining building by way of a lineshaft, a clear example of the windmill as an engine.

The chief centre for the manufacture of white lead was Newcastle upon Tyne, largely because of the suitability of the lead produced by the mines in the Alton Moor area to the west. It was also a town in which industries using white lead had become established. For many centuries it had been an important port and commercial centre; in particular the many staithes along the river shipped large quantities of coal to London and elsewhere. The coal trade spawned two other industries, pot and glass making, the essential ingredients, flint and sand, being imported as ballast in the returning, otherwise empty, coal ships.

The opportunities offered by the white lead trade attracted the Walker brothers, who had started out in 1746 as iron founders at Masborough near Rotherham and were fast becoming the major iron founders in the north of England. In 1778 they entered into partnership with Richard Fishwick and Archer Ward. Both of these partners came from Hull, which was the main port for the transhipment of lead mined in the Peak District. Ward was a merchant dealing in this commodity whilst Fishwick was an expert on the production of lead oxides. The partners built a factory at Elswick on the north bank of the Tyne for the specific purpose of making white lead. The process used at the factory was one perfected by the Dutch, but improved by Fishwick. Small castings of metallic lead were placed in earthenware pots over a little acid. The pots were then immersed in spent tan and placed in a brick chamber called a stack. After about ten to twelve weeks, some 65 per cent of the metallic lead had been converted to lead carbonate, white lead. The powder then needed to be ground in water and dried in a stove, the whole process taking some three months.

To power the grinding mill, the partners built a windmill. There are no pictures of this mill but a valuation held in the Newcastle Local History Library, undated but thought to be about 1800, provides a list of the mill's contents, from which we can deduce how the mill would have appeared. Although there is no mention of bricks, it is quite clear that it was a tower mill, with four sails, a timber upright shaft and wind shaft, but with many parts of both wrought iron (50cwt) and cast iron (18cwt). It had a fantail, almost certainly of the horizontal type. The partners' journal does not specify the date the windmill was built, but it was probably part of the original factory erected in 1778. Alternatively, it is possible that the partners were influenced by Smeaton's later work in Newcastle, on the oil mill at Stepney and the corn mill known as Chimney Mill. We know from the Boulton & Watt Engine book that in 1795 and 1798 steam engines were supplied to the Elswick White Lead Manufactory, and it seems probable that one of these engines took over the task performed by the windmill up to that time, as the windmill was demolished around 1800. It is relevant to note that the Walker brothers had installed their first steam engine, at Masborough, in 1782 but in spite of that they continued with wind power at Newcastle for another 15 years. Although Smeaton had an involvement with the two windmills in the town, at Stepney and Chimney Mill, Newcastle does not receive much attention in the literature on windmills. In fact there is a long history of wind power use, many corn mills being sited on the high ground to the north of the town and on Gateshead Fell to the south of the river. It should also be observed that, during the 18th century, the limited supply of water power available in the area, the Ouseburn, was taken up by several flint mills.

The partnership rapidly expanded their white lead operation and in 1785 opened two further factories, at Finsbury Field, on the boundary between Islington and Shoreditch, and at Red Bull Wharf, also in London. The former factory contained two tower mills, both of similar size, about fifty feet to the curb, with a wide braced stage. One mill had five common sails when built, the other four, but in 1791 the five-sailer was fitted with Hooper's roller sails, which were obviously regarded as a success, as a year later the four-sailer was similarly converted.

The mills were still in operation in the 1820s, being described as 'curious' by a writer in *The Ambulator* of that year. The writer seems to have found it curious that each mill was fitted with a fantail, of the early horizontal type. By the date

22 The white lead mills of Samuel Walker & Co. built at Finsbury Fields in 1786. From a watercolour by Julias Ibbetson, *c.*1795.

of the article the fantail was a common feature; in fact, the mill at Nine Elms, referred to earlier, had a fully developed upright fantail by 1830, which may well have been fitted by 1820. Another perhaps curious feature of the mills was that they both had a bowsprit extending from the front of the windshaft, from which guy ropes were connected to the outer end of each sail. The horizontal fantail was probably similar to that used at the partners' Elswick factory and was certainly used on Chimney Mill, which has caused some speculation that Smeaton was involved in the design of these mills in London. There is no evidence to support this, but it must be quite clear that the partners were well aware of current practice and demanded this at their new mills in London.

One of the mills contained eight pairs of stones for crushing lead and the other may well have also produced linseed oil, an appropriate combination in a mill producing paint. As noted, the mills were still in use in the 1820s, but a few years later they were replaced by a steam engine.

The partners opened other lead mills, one in 1792 at New Normanton, then a village, now a suburb of Derby. We can assume the partners were attracted to this site by its proximity to the Peak District lead mines. Power was needed and, although the mighty River Derwent flows through the town, available water power sites were already fully (and famously) occupied. However, this was no deterrent. The partners' windmills elsewhere had obviously proved to be successful and consequently they were able to select a site away from the river by using wind power. An article in the *Derby Mercury* of 1816 mentions that the windmill was being reduced in height, from which we can assume that the machinery in the mill was to be driven by a steam engine, and the wind engine, i.e. the cap and sails, was being removed. In 1838 the premises were sold to Cox and Company, a local firm who had opened a lead works at Morledge in the centre of Derby in 1781. Cox's continued to operate the works until the 1960s, at which date the lowered mill was still in existence with its machinery, although driven by electric motors. The tower was described as some fifty feet high and about thirty feet in diameter at the base, and retained its upright shaft, two pairs of large diameter horizontal stones and several pairs of smaller stones, still used to grind white lead for use in the manufacture of paint. Thus, this mill would appear to have been in continuous operation for almost two hundred years, being powered first by wind engine, then by steam engine and finally by electric motors.

Turning now to the pigments, a wide variety of minerals was used, it being said of one paint maker that he '... made dull earths and mineral poisons to give out and yield up to him colours as rich as those of the solar rainbow'. The paint maker was Henry Blundell of Hull, who in 1811 founded the firm of Blundell and Spence. Their first factory was on Beverley Road, a site which included a five-sail tower mill built as a corn mill in 1788 by James Norman before he entered into partnership with Robert Smithson. Substantial new buildings were erected on the site, including two steam engines, but wind power continued to be used until 1846.

The earliest wind-powered paint mills are found in Liverpool, a port which, although it had a limited amount of water power available, relied heavily upon wind power in the 18th century. Bennett and Elton (*History of Corn Milling*) explain that, once the soke of milling had been abolished in 1689, private landowners started to build their own windmills. The new mills, which the authors describe as 'squat towers', were generally on the high ground to the east of the town but one stood to the north, close to the foreshore, and it is in this latter area that a second tranche of new windmills was built around 1770, an area adjacent to the Leeds-Liverpool Canal.

Liverpool's first historian, William Enfield (*An Essay towards the History of Liverpool* – published in 1773) writes that in 1770, 'There are in or very near to the town of Leverpool [*sic*] 27 Wind – Mills; of which 16 are for grinding corn, 9 for grinding colours, & C. one for rasping and grinding dyer's wood, and one for raising water at the salt works.'

Enfield also produced a map of the town as it stood in 1768, which is reproduced by Bennet and Elton (Vol.4), on which are shown the sites of 27 windmills. Unfortunately, Enfield has omitted from his map the site of the windmill at the salt works, so we have an inconsistency. (This mill is mentioned in a later chapter.) We also know that in 1770 there was one mill, possibly two, crushing linseed, which is not specifically mentioned in Enfield's text. However, Bennett and Elton do identify one of the mills on the map as an oil mill.

So there is some confusion, which has been compounded by subsequent writers who have quoted Enfield's statement set out above, but who have omitted

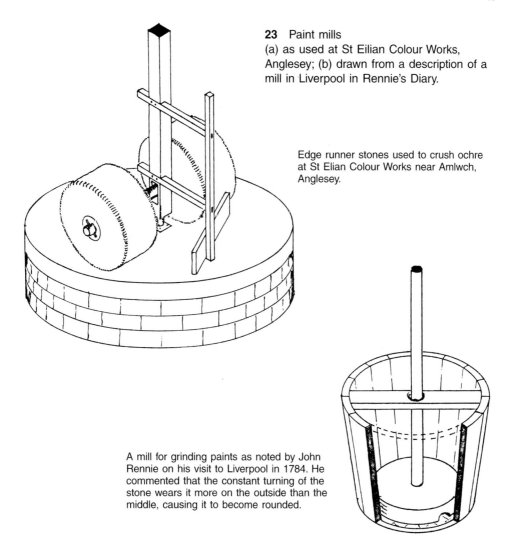

23 Paint mills
(a) as used at St Eilian Colour Works,
Anglesey; (b) drawn from a description of a
mill in Liverpool in Rennie's Diary.

Edge runner stones used to crush ochre
at St Elian Colour Works near Amlwch,
Anglesey.

A mill for grinding paints as noted by John
Rennie on his visit to Liverpool in 1784. He
commented that the constant turning of the
stone wears it more on the outside than the
middle, causing it to become rounded.

the '& C.', giving the impression that the nine mills were all for grinding colour. Bennett and Elton devote several pages to the 27 mills shown on the map but, although they have spotted the oil mill, they give no indication that any of the windmills was used for grinding colours. A perusal of the trade directories for the period 1768 to 1787 has failed to provide any further information.

The author suggests that when Enfield used the words '9 for grinding colours, & C.' he was referring to mills used to produce paint, which would include both the colours and the linseed oil, and that one (possibly two) oil mill was included in the figure of nine. The location of the colour mills is therefore in some doubt but it seems likely to have been to the north of the old town, the area around the Leeds and Liverpool Canal, which was being promoted during the 1760s. Enfield would, of course, have had personal knowledge of these mills so we can be sure they existed, but we cannot be sure of how many there were, nor their precise location.

As for the internal machinery, we shall see below that wood was also used as a source of pigment. As Enfield differentiates this from 'colour' grinding, it can be assumed that the nine colour mills were crushing 'dull earths and / or mineral poisons'. Indeed, we have a detailed account of the internal machinery used in one of them, through the diary of John Rennie, who records that he visited a 'mill for grinding paints' at Liverpool in May 1784. He describes the machine as follows:

> This machine has an upright shaft with a spur wheel on its lower end round which is [a ring of] tubs for holding the paints & to each of these tubs is adapted a spindle that turns round a large stone in their bottom; ... the tub whose bottom is laid with hard stones & their [sic] is a large stone ... with a hole in it to which the spindle is fastened so as to turn it round. The stone has also a semi-circular groove cut across below its middle to allow the paints to get in their [sic]. By the constant turning of the stone it wears more on the outside than the middle & at last it becomes of a circular form [i.e. convex]. There is also adapted to this mill a tub as the former but much larger, with a frame at [the bottom] exactly like a set of arms of a wheel thats laid round the axle & there is a pump adjoining which raises water to soften the clay so that by the turning of the arms amongst the water & clay it is at last made into a soft substance like [Sowans].

The machine last described sounds like what we today would call a blunger, which is used at potteries for mixing the slop to the required consistency and holding it in that state until required for pot making. It is assumed that it was not used for this purpose here. The reference to clay may indicate that the mill was grinding ochre (discussed below) and that the 'blunger' was used to keep the colour in suspension until despatched to customers.

As for the external appearance of these mills, we have no specific evidence, but we do have evidence of the general style of windmill erected in Liverpool at the time of Rennie's visit. He records that he saw many windmills in Liverpool '... but their construction was so like that at Preston that it is unnecessary to detail these'.

In Preston he saw a 'pretty large mill' for grinding flour and oat meal which he describes as a brick tower mill, five storeys high, with a gallery and winding wheel and fitted with four common sails. This description matches a windmill shown in an engraving of the Wishing Gate Mill, a corn mill which is known to have existed in Liverpool by 1785, and a drawing of Pickup's Mill at the corner of Love Lane and Chisenhale Street of similar date. This design was common in Lancashire and it is more than likely that the colour mills were of this design. A later painting by S.F. Serres (1799) of the Liverpool foreshore shows a large seven-storey windmill fitted with a horizontal fantail, which is probably the replacement Townside Mill, built around 1785, but it is rather surprising that Liverpool millwrights seem to have been slow to adopt the fantail.

Also in Lancashire, a three-storey brick tower mill, built at Lancaster before 1786 to grind corn, was used during the 19th century to grind colours for a pottery on the Quay. In this case it seems likely that the colour grinding was carried out using a pair of cast-iron rollers.

A wind-powered paint mill was built at Ashley, near Ashbourne, in the 1830s. It is not clear what raw materials were being used, but it is known that the limestone measures produced material for use as a pigment. For example, stone from the quarries at Froghall was used to produce a red oxide called 'cherry eye'. The windmill at Ashley was described as a spacious brick tower with sails and fantail, the domed cap being covered with zinc sheet. The internal machinery comprised two pairs of edge runner stones, two mixers, five pairs of colour stones and four pairs of paint stones, a hand crane and two iron pumps. In fact, the mill had a very short life, as in 1847 it was advertised for sale and demolished shortly afterwards. Interestingly, it is also recorded that the mill drove an associated tobacco-processing plant, but what this comprised is not recorded.

Here again we meet the phrase 'colour stones', in this case differentiated from 'paint stones'. So far enquiries have failed to produce a definitive explanation of the difference between these two types of stones. The best guess is that one type could be edge runner stones, the other the arrangement described by John Rennie.

The 'earth' used to produce pigments was ochre, a clay containing iron oxide and which produces pigments ranging from yellow to red, dependent upon the percentage of the oxide present. An important deposit of ochre was found in the eastern part of Oxfordshire, which was claimed to be 'a very superior sort', producing a very bright yellow paint. It is also claimed that the material was exported as far away as China. In this case, three existing corn mills were adapted to crush the ochre, the work probably being carried out under contract for local firms who dug the local ochre pits.

The first was at Little Milton, a three-storey tower mill with a conical cap, four common sails and winded by winding wheel. It was out of use before the end of the 19th century and demolished in 1910. The second was sited at South Weston. Rebuilt in 1852, it was a low octagonal smock mill with four common sails and winded by tailpole. One writer has described the mill as rather ugly, no doubt because of the rather large pent roof cap which seems totally out of proportion to the rest of the structure. Neither of these mills could be described as state-of-the-art. Oxfordshire was very much watermill territory, which outnumbered windmills by something like three to one.

However, the third windmill was a more substantial structure, namely Wheatley Mill. Built in 1784, it was a tower mill of local stone but of an unusual shape, being octagonal at ground-floor level, merging to circular in plan at the second floor. This may well be a case of an 18th-century millwright trying to build a mill in the style of the newfangled smock mill but using vernacular materials. Internally, the upright shaft and gears are of timber, as is the windshaft, although the sail stocks, instead of being mortised through the outer end of the windshaft, are held in a cast-iron canister bearing the legend 'Eagle Foundry 1784'.

The mill was built to grind corn, the stones being underdriven (i.e., the spur wheel on the upright shaft was fixed below the stones), an arrangement more common in watermills than windmills. The ochre crushing plant was located outside the tower, driven by a belt from a vertical shaft which meshed with the spur wheel. The plant is shown in a photograph to be a cast-iron frame with at least one, probably two, large cast-iron rollers, about four feet in diameter and twelve to eighteen inches in width.

When this mill was built (1784), the fantail was only just emerging from its infancy, being developed by millwrights in the north of England. That is not to say that this millwright was not also enterprising – quite the reverse. He eschewed the tail pole and wind wheel, constructing a clever hand crank arrangement for winding the mill, operated from inside the cap. Instead of the usual 'dead' curb, where small cast-iron blocks (pigs) set into the underside of the cap frame simply slide round on the cast-iron curb, he placed small truck wheels between the two (a 'live' curb), which no doubt made the task of turning the cap using the hand crank a much easier operation. At a later stage, one of the enterprising millers improved matters further by adding a fantail to drive the crank automatically.

24 Wheatley Windmill, near Oxford, built in 1784 as a corn mill, with ochre crushing plant located outside the tower, added during the mid-19th century. The plant was driven by a belt from a layshaft inside the tower.

The mill continued in business until 1939, at which date the sails were destroyed by lightning. Fortunately the mill is now in the care of a trust which is undertaking a thorough restoration and the mill should be producing flour within the foreseeable future. Unfortunately, the cast-iron plant used to crush ochre has not been found, probably long gone to some scrap metal merchant.

Another major source of ochre occurred as a by-product from the enormous copper mine near Amlwch on Anglesey. By 1850 the St Eilian Colour Works were in business producing ochre, Venetian red and umber. An advertisement of 1889 claimed that '... the product was a strong, brilliant yellow, soft and free from impurities ... the golden hue presented by the paper hanging of the best makers in England'.

Guise and Lees (*Windmills in Anglesey*) describe the process. The mineral-rich water issuing out of the mine workings was channelled into long, shallow pits, filled with pieces of scrap iron. After a time some of the iron dissolved, to be replaced by copper oxide, which produced a red pigment. The water was heavily impregnated with iron sulphate and, on being allowed to run off slowly, exposed to the air the sulphate precipitated as hydrated iron oxide, which, as we have seen, produces yellow ochre. The material was crushed using a windmill.

Crushing was achieved somewhat differently from the method used in Liverpool and Oxfordshire, using edge runner stones. Until recently, several stones remained on site; they were some 26 inches in diameter and 12 inches thick. The windmill was demolished many years ago but we can assume that it was similar to other mills on Anglesey, having four common sails and winded by chain wheel. The mill was situated in an excellent area for the application of wind power, as is testified by the nearby modern wind farm.

Finally, as far as paint mills are concerned, an edition of the *Hull Advertiser* in 1816 carries an advertisement which claimed that one Robert Dawson had patented a horizontal windmill, an example of which he had erected at Witham in the town for grinding paint. The patent recorded in Dawson's name (Patent No 3463, 3 July 1811) is a variation of the Chinese version of the horizontal windmill, with a sort of self-regulating gadget, but it is likely to have provided very little power and nothing more is heard of the mill in Hull.

Several organic materials were used to produce pigments, two in particular being Brazil wood and Logwood. Brazil, or redwood, was originally imported from Asia by the Arabs who transported it along the silk roads. It is claimed that the wood derived its name from the Arabic word 'braza' which means fiery red. Later, when the Portuguese entered the country we now know as Brazil, they found this timber growing there in abundance, hence the name. Thereafter, Brazil became the prime source of redwood. Logwood, also known as compeachy wood after Compeachy Bay in Mexico where it was first found, reached Europe in 1519 and was later imported from Honduras, Jamaica, Haiti and Brazil. Logwood produced a blue pigment. To convert logs into a form in which it could be used as pigment, two special types of machine were used, dependent upon the nature of the wood. The first was a 'chipper' in which the end of the log was pressed against a circular plate to which were attached four knives. As the plate rotated the knives chipped away slivers of the wood. The second device was the 'rasper' where the log was pressed against a barrel, which was in effect a large rasp. There are designs for both of these machines amongst the Smeaton Drawings in the Royal Society Library and an example of a chipper, dating from the 1870s, can be seen at Albert Mill, Keynsham. After chipping or rasping, the resultant material would be further reduced under edge runner stones.

As might be expected, the mills were located either at the ports of entry or at sites with access to the ports by water. The earliest windmill to be used to produce colours from imported wood stood at Barking in Essex, immediately adjacent to Barking Creek, a site which Kenneth Farries (*Essex Windmills*) describes as 'favourable for the receipt of water-borne supplies of timber and dyewoods'. The mill was probably a smock mill built around 1738, which contained one pair of peak stones, two rasping barrels, a chipper and a pair of edge runner stones. Sometime between 1753 and 1780 John Smeaton had an involvement with this mill and it is thought he may well have remodelled the internal plant; he certainly included the mill in a list of 'mills executed' which he compiled in 1780. The mill had been demolished by 1805.

Next is the mill at Wakefield, which was built to Smeaton's design in 1754 and has already been described in the chapter on oil seed crushing. Shortly after it was built he also designed a rasper and chipper to be installed in the mill. As has been noted, Wakefield was connected to the port of Hull by the Aire and Calder Navigation.

An interesting dyewood mill operated in Manchester which, in 1700, was a small town standing on a rocky promontory at the confluence of the Rivers Irwell

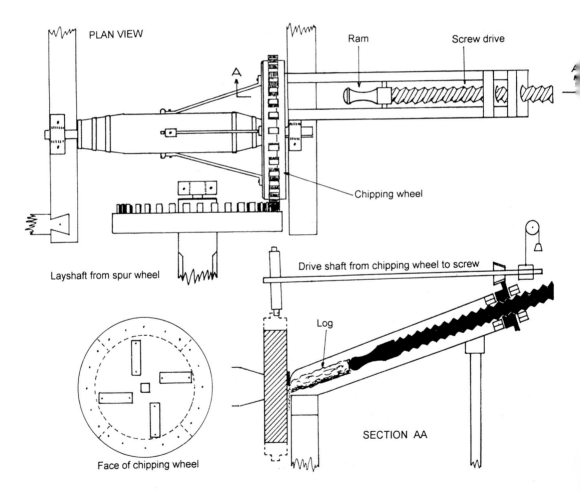

25 Diagram of a dyewood chipping engine (after John Smeaton).

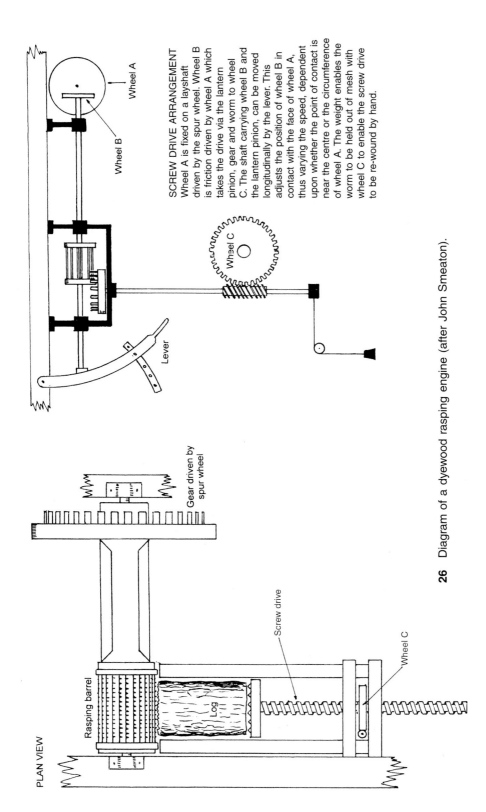

SCREW DRIVE ARRANGEMENT
Wheel A is fixed on a layshaft driven by the spur wheel. Wheel B is friction driven by wheel A which takes the drive via the lantern pinion, gear and worm to wheel C. The shaft carrying wheel B and the lantern pinion, can be moved longitudinally by the lever. This adjusts the position of wheel B in contact with the face of wheel A, thus varying the speed, dependent upon whether the point of contact is near the centre or the circumference of wheel A. The weight enables the worm to be held out of mesh with wheel C to enable the screw drive to be re-wound by hand.

Wheel A

Wheel B

Wheel C

Lever

PLAN VIEW

Gear driven by spur wheel

Rasping barrel

Log

Screw drive

Wheel C

26 Diagram of a dyewood rasping engine (after John Smeaton).

and Irk, the latter providing power for the town's two mills. An advertisement in the *Manchester Mercury* of 1766 refers to a windmill 'at the top of Deansgate', equipped with four pairs of stones for grinding all sorts of dying wood and pot ashes, two grindle stones and two rasping mills. This mill was principally producing dyes for the textile industry, but at the same time there must have been a demand for paint in an area where heavy engineering was becoming established. The source of raw materials is not known. At this date the Manchester Ship Canal was not even a pipe dream but work on the Duke of Bridgewater's canal from his mines at Worsley to the centre of Manchester was well under way and the Act of Parliament authorising the extension to Runcorn had already been granted (in 1762). The mill in Deansgate was extremely close to the Manchester basin of the canal at Castlefield, and access to the canal may have been a factor when the site was selected. The mill was quite a successful venture and continued in operation until at least 1811, the site being still acknowledged in the name Windmill Street behind the old Free Trade Hall.

We know very little else about the mill, apart from one matter, which tends to be ignored – John Smeaton had an involvement with this mill. Amongst his papers in the Royal Society Library is a note (probably dating from *c*.1754) which reads:

> A cross that is layd into a wooden shaft one which was used by Mr Taylor of Manchester and another by Mr Pease of Hull about 5ft long with the cross at the head an T at the tail, 9 inches in the neck and tapering backwards. Weight 26 cwt …

This clearly indicates that a cast-iron cross was added to the wooden windshaft.

There is no firm evidence to tie Mr Taylor's mill with the mill at Deansgate, but the trade directory for 1781 includes a Charles Taylor who is described as a Manufacturer, Printer and Dyer. In the absence of any other known windmills in Manchester, it must be a distinct possibility, particularly as this was an industrial mill.

We can now turn briefly to Liverpool, the major port for trade with the New World. We have already seen that Enfield noted a dyewood mill in 1770, but sadly nothing else is known about it.

Finally we return to London, to the western side where two water-powered dyewood mills were in operation at Hounslow on the River Crane and at Wandsworth on the River Wandle. By the beginning of the 19th century, the tributaries of the Thames in the vicinity of the capital were occupied by over five hundred watermills, contributing to the wide range of products required to meet the demands of the inhabitants. In these two cases the mill owners wished to increase their output, which needed additional power, and this was achieved by adding a windmill to each mill, a more economic option than a steam engine. The windmill added at Wandsworth was a large smock mill with four common sails; the windmill at Hounslow was probably similar.

5

Crushing Stone and Clay

Chalk

Chalk is a white calcareous fine-grained rock, laid down in the cretaceous period, which forms the top solid geological strata in the south-east of England. It can be found, generally speaking, south-east of a line drawn from Portland Bill in Dorset to Flamborough Head in East Yorkshire, producing the geographic features known as the Downs and the Wolds. Chalk has been quarried at many places in that region and used in its simple quarried form for civil engineering purposes, e.g. road building, as a back-fill for dock construction, etc.

Several quarries also produced whiting. Whilst not exactly a sideline, in the early 19th century it was usually a small percentage of a quarry's output. Whiting was produced by crushing lumps of chalk in water and then allowing the slurry to overflow into a settling pit, where impurities – sand, flint and the like – settled out. The resulting slurry was then pumped along a second series of settling pits (between eight and twelve) which provided a system of grading, the larger particles settling out first, the finest last. The water was then drained off and the settled-out material was lifted out of the pits in blocks and dried in sheds, the walls of which were characteristically fitted with louvred shutters, which could be adjusted according to weather conditions. Whiting has a number of uses – mixed with linseed oil it produces putty, in paint, as an 'extender' in a whole range of goods, e.g. rubber boots, and the finest grade is the basis for toothpaste and cosmetics.

Although whiting was frequently produced at chalk quarries, in fact the earliest reference to a whiting mill occurs not at a quarry but at a site on the River Hull, appropriately named Stoneferry. It appears to have been built between 1775 and 1790 and comprised a medium height brick tower which, by c.1830, had been fitted with five roller sails and an upright fantail. As there is no evidence of a quarry in the immediate neighbourhood it is likely that the raw material was brought by barge from one of the several quarries along the Humber estuary.

Where the estuary cuts through the Wolds, there were a number of quarries on each bank. The next known whiting mill stood at Barton on the south bank. It was offered for sale in 1804 as a combined wind and horse mill, the horse mill producing Spanish whiting and the windmill, a brick tower mill, producing Paris whiting. The windmill was demolished in 1946 but another whiting mill, still stands in the Market Place at Barton. It was built in 1810 for Thomas Marris and fitted with six sails but, following Marris' death in 1815, it was advertised as being 'lately fitted up' with millstones for grinding corn. This mill was poorly sited for whiting manufacture, being in the centre of the village some way from the nearest quarry, and it must have been something of a speculation on the part of Marris. The mill tower survives and is now converted to a restaurant. By 1829 two further whiting mills had been built south of the Humber, both brick tower mills, known respectively as Bank Mill and Kingsforth Mill, the latter being a little to the south of the village. Finally, a wind-powered oil mill at West Ferry, built during the latter part of the 18th century, was also set up to produce whiting but it is not entirely clear whether the whiting mill was driven by wind or by horse gin.

Directly across the estuary from Barton lies the village of Hessle, where chalk has been quarried since medieval times, an early use being the production of quick lime for agricultural purposes. In the 18th century a number of kilns for this purpose stood in the quarry. Being adjacent to the Humber, the quarry had its own jetties for loading material into barges and an internal tramway system. From the late 18th century onwards output expanded rapidly and the quarry also commenced the production of whiting, at first using a horse mill. A circular iron plate preserved on site is reputed to have been part of the horse mill. The horse mill was built in 1796 but within a few years (possibly as early as 1803 but certainly before 1812) it was replaced by a substantial brick tower mill, seven storeys high, with an ogee cap, gallows fantail, five roller sails and a braced stage. Externally it was identical in appearance to the oil mill built at Stoneferry in 1791 by Norman and Smithson and it is reasonable to conclude that Hessle Whiting Mill was built by that firm. This conclusion may well be supported by the fact that Pinning (one of the proprietors who built the horse mill) worked with Norman in 1803, when Pinning supplied stone for the new Ferry Boat Dock in Hull being built by Norman. It is on record that Norman visited the quarry to discuss financial terms with Pinning and it is not difficult to envisage him observing the horse mill and quietly pointing out that some of Pinning's competitors used wind power.

The quarry continued in operation until the 1960s and the wind-powered complex was still extant in the 1970s, although much of it had been vandalised. The complex was built round a courtyard. The east range contained the sand pit and a bank of eight settling pits. The south range comprised a single-storey drying shed. The north range was a two-storeyed building, with a drying shed at first-floor level. The ground floor contained a well, a second bank of eight settling pits and a raised stone flagged floor, heated from below like a Roman hypocaust, which could be used for the quick drying of the settled material. The fire box for the heated floor was in the western range, together with an office. The mill tower was situated in the north-east corner, between the two ranges containing settling tanks.

Inside the tower, the upright shaft (the lower half of which survives) is of pine with a cast-iron spur wheel at its lower end. This engaged with a large stone

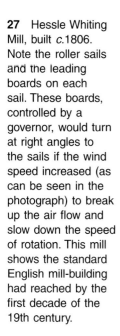

27 Hessle Whiting Mill, built c.1806. Note the roller sails and the leading boards on each sail. These boards, controlled by a governor, would turn at right angles to the sails if the wind speed increased (as can be seen in the photograph) to break up the air flow and slow down the speed of rotation. This mill shows the standard English mill-building had reached by the first decade of the 19th century.

nut, which unfortunately has been smashed off, but it would appear that the gear ratio was at least a 2-1 step-down in speed. At the lower end of the shaft driven by the stone nut, a pair of edge runner stones (5ft 1ins in diameter) turned in a wooden tub (8ft 6ins in diameter) on an axle held by the shaft in a vertical slot, to allow the stones to rise and fall as they moved over different sized lumps of chalk. The stones were originally fitted with iron tyres, held in place by wooden wedges, which expanded when the stones turned in water to ensure a tight fit.

The mill continued in use under wind power until the sails were removed in 1925, due to the fact that the canvas rollers suffered frequent damage and the owner found it difficult to replace them. However, that was not the end of the operation, as a new and larger tub was constructed on the ground floor with much larger diameter stones, driven from below by gears and shafts from an electric motor

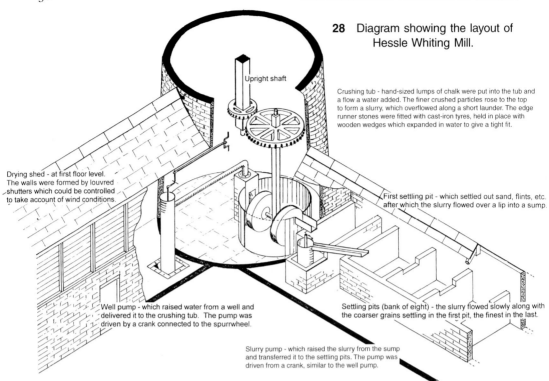

28 Diagram showing the layout of Hessle Whiting Mill.

Upright shaft

Crushing tub - hand-sized lumps of chalk were put into the tub and a flow a water added. The finer crushed particles rose to the top to form a slurry, which overflowed along a short launder. The edge runner stones were fitted with cast-iron tyres, held in place with wooden wedges which expanded in water to give a tight fit.

Drying shed - at first floor level. The walls were formed by louvred shutters which could be controlled to take account of wind conditions.

First settling pit - which settled out sand, flints, etc. after which the slurry flowed over a lip into a sump.

Well pump - which raised water from a well and delivered it to the crushing tub. The pump was driven by a crank connected to the spurrwheel.

Settling pits (bank of eight) - the slurry flowed slowly along with the coarser grains settling in the first pit, the finest in the last.

Slurry pump - which raised the slurry from the sump and transferred it to the settling pits. The pump was driven from a crank, similar to the well pump.

29 Edge runner stones in Hessle Whiting Mill. The stones have lost their cast-iron tyres, which would have been held in place by wooden wedges.

installed in a pit below the level of the new tub. To install the larger stones in the mill it was necessary to cut a vertical slot in the side of the mill. At the time preservation works were carried out in the 1980s these stones had disappeared and the slot was bricked up. They have since been recovered but cannot at present be reinstated in the mill; consequently they are now outside the tower, arranged as a landscape feature.

Further north along the Wolds, some ten miles from Hessle, three chalk quarries were opened at Beverley in the 19th century, one of which, the Victoria works, had a wind-powered whiting mill. Built in 1837 by Robert Garton of Beverley, it was again a large brick tower mill, the base being 27 feet in diameter, fitted with five sails. There was the usual range of drying sheds attached to the tower. The main use of the windmill was to drive machinery in the whiting works but the mill was also fitted with three pairs of grey mill stones. It is unlikely that grey stones would have been used to produce flour at that date. Is it possible that

30 Beverley Whiting Mill, built in 1837. Note the drying shed with louvred sides.

these stones were intended to produce animal feed for the horses which the quarry operator must have used for quarry work and for deliveries? The Crawthorne family sold the quarry and the mill to the owner of one of the adjoining quarries in 1895. It seems likely, therefore, that Crawthorne's purchase was intended as an investment, as the quarry continued as such during his ownership. Indeed, the combined quarries are still in operation today and the truncated tower of the windmill remains on site.

Moving southwards along the chalk strata, away from the Humber estuary, we come to Brandon in Suffolk where *White's Directory* of 1844 includes three whiting mills along the Thetford Road. The earliest, shown as a windmill on the 1838 Tithe map, stood on land named 'New Mill Place', from which it can be assumed that the mill was recently built, the owner/occupier being named James Green. In 1844 Green was described as a 'joiner, builder and cabinet maker' and it has been suggested that he may have been extracting chalk and producing whiting for building purposes. The other two mills mentioned in 1844 were erected after the date of the Tithe map and it is assumed they were steam driven. The windmill had disappeared by 1882.

Cambridgeshire also had a wind-powered whiting mill, at Linton. Built in *c*.1820, it comprised a small tower mill of individual design. A photograph of late 19th-century date shows the cap to be a six-sided pyramid. There were four single-sided common sails, the stocks being held in a cast-iron canister, which had a bowsprit, extending some five or six feet, from the end of which a stay was connected to the end of each sail. But the most unusual feature was the tailpole, the angle of which appears to be only a few degrees greater than that of the windshaft, resulting in the outer end being totally out of reach by anyone on the ground. Consequently, to enable the cap to be turned, a rope was attached to the outer end, which the operator would pull. The reason for this arrangement may lie in the fact that the mill stood immediately adjacent to the GER track from Cambridge to Colchester, which at this point was on a modest embankment. A tail pole at a normal angle would certainly make the operator walk on the

31 Linton Whiting Mill, built *c.*1820.

32 Rudmore Whiting Mill, built by 1823.

embankment and, even if this was practical, it is hard to imagine the Railway Company sanctioning it. So a compromise seems to have been reached, the tail pole being allowed to overhang the railway boundary fence (but clear of the actual track) which had to be activated, using the rope, from within the mill boundary. By 1929, the use of wind power had been discontinued and the crushing tub was driven by an external belt drive from a steam engine. The tower was taken down to first-floor level and a circular tank constructed as a roof, probably to store water for use in the crushing process.

Finally, down in Hampshire, a booklet published by Anthony Triggs, a local journalist, suggests that a mill at Rudmore, on the edge of Portsmouth Harbour, sometimes called Byerly Mill, may have been used at some stage for crushing lime. Triggs recognises that the provenance is doubtful, being based on a watercolour in the Portsmouth Museum collection, entitled *Rudmore Lime Mill*. Contemporary maps show this as a corn mill but two lime kilns stood next to the mill and are shown in the painting, and it is possible that this misled the artist. In the painting, the kilns are shown uncomfortably close to the mill and, in certain weather conditions, smoke and fumes must have entered the higher floors of the mill. The tower has a very wide stage at first-floor level but without any handrail, and a crude ladder from the stage leads to a door at second-floor level. This must have been inconvenient at best and may indicate that the internal layout had been altered at some time. The sails seem to be double patent sails, whilst a platform at the rear of the cap appears to hold a chain wheel and some unrecognisable arrangement for adjusting the sails.

There was at least one lime kiln, in the Isle of Man, which had a wind-scoop to provide an induced draft, but details of its construction have not been found.

Cement

Chalk was certainly used to produce cement, but two mills are known to have produced cement obtaining the raw material from a different source.

The first is at Berney Arms on the River Yare, shortly before it enters Brey-don Water. Cement has been produced at this site since the 18th century, using the chalky mud dredged from the river. The present mill, built *c*.1856, comprises a tall tower mill, some 70 feet to the top of the cap, with an internal diameter at ground level of 28 feet. The cap is the

33 Burney Arms Mill, built *c*.1856.

typical Norfolk boat shape and has four double-sided patent sails and fantail. In 1880 cement grinding ceased and the mill was converted to a drainage mill using a 34 foot diameter scoop wheel.

Unfortunately, the cement grinding equipment was removed during conversion but there is a limited amount of evidence still available. Two millstones survive, which the English Heritage leaflet states were used as edge runner stones. The two stones have been stacked one on top of the other, which makes a full examination difficult, but it is possible to discern the remains of a dress and scouring on the face, which suggests that the stones may have been mounted and used horizontally. There is certainly a precedent for this; for example, such an arrangement was used at Lode Watermill in Cambridgeshire. At Berney Arms, the stones appear to have been located at second-floor level, which is unusual in stone crushing mills, and there must have been some form of elevator to raise the raw material to this level. There could be a good reason for the stones being located at this point. One might expect the crushed material to require some form of screening process to remove unwanted material, or simply to grade the particles, and the logical place for this would be on the first floor, underneath the stones, with the screened or graded material being bagged up on the ground floor.

English Heritage have restored the mill, in its last working form, as a drainage mill, and it stands as a magnificent feature in the Broads landscape.

A second cement mill stood at Woodbridge in Suffolk, on the River Deben. It is assumed that this mill also used material dredged from the river. It comprised a tower mill with patent sails and fantail, and was probably built by a local millwright, Henry Collins, whose yard was about a mile away at Melton. This mill perhaps demonstrates some of the problems faced by users of wind power, first in 1841 when it was tail-winded in a storm and lost three sails. Secondly, following repair, it was struck by lightning. The premises seem to have gone out of use shortly after 1852.

Gypsum

Gypsum is in demand for the production of plaster of Paris. During the course of the process the raw material requires grinding, which was achieved using burr millstones, the method used by British Gypsum up until 1990. There were several water-powered mills in Staffordshire producing this material, one of which stood at Tutbury near Derby. The mill buildings have been demolished and the area of the mill turned into a recreation area. However, a pair of burr millstones can still be seen on site, set up as a feature in the park. In the 1830/40s, a deposit of gypsum was found in the Isle of Axholme and it is believed that, from time to time, a batch of the raw material was ground using any available local mill, the stones being simply cleaned out after use. There were several windmills in this area, which could have been used in this way, but to date there is no confirmation of this.

34 Bassingbourn Coprolite Mills.

Coprolites

Coprolites are the fossilised nodules of the excrement of animals. Fish coprolites occur in the cretaceous beds of Cambridgeshire where they formed a source of phosphates used for fertilisers. Before the fossilised remains could be used, it was of course necessary to reduce the stone to powder form. During the 1850s at Burwell and Bassingbourn, existing corn windmills were taken over and used for this purpose. It is not known what type of plant was used. Edge runner stones would be an obvious possibility although at this late date it may well be that cast-iron rollers were used.

The mill at Burwell was a large tower mill built in 1812 to grind corn. It was subsequently damaged in a storm, as a consequence of which it was reduced to a three-storey structure. About 1850 it was used to grind coprolites but appears to have reverted to corn milling during the 1880s, possibly due to the opening at that date of a large fertiliser factory nearby. The stump of the tower still survives, in use as a farm store.

A most interesting coprolite works operated at Bassingbourn (also called Kneesworth Mills), to the south-west of Cambridge. It comprised a small industrial complex with a range of outbuildings and an internal railway system. Power was provided by three windmills, a post mill and two tower mills. The complex was owned by Nunn's in the 1880s, before which it had been used to grind corn. The post mill was an amalgam of different regional styles. The buck was the Midlands and North Eastern type, whereby the round house roof turned with the buck, whereas the fantail was attached to the outer end of the tail pole, as found in early mills in Norfolk and Sussex. It had four single-sided spring sails. The post mill was out of use by 1903.

The two tower mills were of similar height, about fifty feet to the curb, but had interesting differences in detail. The first had a tall ogee cap which came well down over the corbelling which held the curb ring. The sails were double-sided patents but with only two shutters per bay and mounted on stocks held in a canister. The second had a slightly different ogee cap and, although the sails had a similar number of shutters per bay, there were two significant differences. First, the sails were not carried on stocks but fixed to a cast-iron cross. Secondly, the up-longs, timber poles which open and close the shutters, ran centrally down the shutters, not immediately adjacent to the sail back, as is usual. The different methods of fixing the sails to the windshaft probably indicate different building dates, that with the cast-iron cross probably being the later of the two.

The three mills were extremely close together and the post mill in particular can only have been used when the wind was blowing from a limited range of directions.

Coal
During the mid-20th century, a cheap form of fuel for domestic purposes was devised, comprising a mixture of coal dust and bitumen, in the form of the coalbrick. One enterprising concern used Werringham corn mill in Staffordshire for this purpose. It is conceivable that normal millstones were used, or some form of small roller mill could have been installed for the purpose. Either way this nicely illustrates the versatility of the windmill. The tower still survives, now used as an electricity substation.

Emery
In the late 18th century, the manufacture of glass was emerging as a major industry in Warrington. Around 1812 the British Plate Glass Works took over a farm mill, built c.1783, which they reportedly used to grind emery for polishing glass until 1832, at which time it was replaced by a steam engine (rated at 10hp). Again, an interesting example of the versatility of the windmill.

Clay for Brickmaking
We have looked in detail at the crushing of clay for the production of ceramics. An industry which has a similar requirement for clay – which had to be dug, crushed and mixed, shaped and fired – is the production of bricks. A wide variety of different clays has been used and in this case it is usual to leave the clay in its natural colour. During the 18th century clay was dug and shaped by hand but

prepared for use with the aid of a pug mill driven by a horse. The pug mill comprised a tub, inside which a vertical shaft with a spiral of projecting horizontal knives was rotated by a horse, walking round the tub, harnessed to the end of a horizontal beam fixed to the top of the vertical shaft. Clay was fed into the top of the tub which was then kneaded by the knives and extruded at the bottom. An excellent example can be seen in the Weald and Downland Museum at Singleton in Sussex.

The earliest known use of wind power to drive a pug mill, as a replacement for the horse, occurred at Crawley in Bedfordshire. Built around 1800, the mill was yet another version of the horizontal mill and is shown in a picture by Thomas Fisher (*c*.1820). The mill is described by Hugh Howes:

35 Crawley horizontal windmill, built *c*.1800. Detail from a drawing by Thomas Fisher.

The sails consisted of a number of pivoted shutters set in a horizontal revolving cylinder so as to catch the wind on one side only. One side flapped open to allow the wind to blow past whilst the opposite shutter blew closed to present a sail area to the wind. This arrangement was attached to a vertical shaft which emerged through the apex of a conical roof.

This appears to be identical to the type of windmill used in China to pump water, and looks very much like Dawson's patent mentioned in connection with a paint mill in Hull. It is difficult to be precise from the painting and the Crawley building date of 1800 would in any case pre-date Dawson's patent. The designer of the mill at Crawley is not recorded but it may have been promoted by the Duke of Bedford who was keen on applying technological novelties on his estates. As with other horizontal mills, it was short-lived and was probably demolished by 1840.

Around Newcastle upon Tyne, at least one, possibly two, standard tower mills were used at brickworks. Towards the end of the 18th century the town was starting to expand and several small adjacent villages were developed with streets of terraced houses, for which large quantities of bricks were required. Most of the villages seemed to have a suitable supply of clay, and brickworks sprang up wherever bricks were required. One such village was Shieldfield, where, in the 1830s, an existing corn windmill, probably dating from the last quarter of the 18th century, was converted to crush clay for an emerging brick and tile business.

An undated picture of the mill, in the
Newcastle Local History Library, shows
it as a three-storey tower mill with a
domed cap, four sails and a horizontal
fantail. At ground-floor level, the tower
was surrounded by a rectangular brick
structure, which may have formed
loading bays for horse-drawn carts. The
sails were most likely commons, as it is
reported that in 1809 the miller narrowly
escaped death when he climbed one
of the sail frames to adjust the cloth,
but the brake failed to hold and the
mill started to turn. The poor chap
made several revolutions before being
rescued. The mill had disappeared by
1856, having been subsumed into the surrounding housing development.

36 Shieldfield Brickworks, Newcastle upon
Tyne, converted in the 1830s.

The second brickworks mill in the town is one which may have existed some
three-quarters of a mile to the east, where the 1858 OS map shows a circular
structure marked 'clay mill' situate at another brick and tile works. Although it
seems about the same size as other windmills marked on the map, in the absence
of a specific legend one can only make an assumption.

From about 1820 onwards, many new devices were patented for making
bricks, one of which was a pan mill for crushing either wet or dry clay. By this date
the steam engine had become a cost effective power source and much of the new
machinery was driven by steam. But one J.A. Woods, who opened a brickworks
at Hornsea on the East Yorkshire coast in 1865, decided to use wind power. The
mill was a tall brick tower mill, fitted with five patent sails and a fantail, and was
also used to pump water out of the pit and to power a tramway incline. The site
of this mill was ideal for the use of wind power, being located in an area where
wind power was well established, and it carried on working for some forty years
until eventually replaced by steam.

There are two possible references to the use of water power at brickworks
in Wales. The first is a little uncertain, being to a brickworks at Llwydiarth
Fawr on Anglesey, an area with a long history of using wind power. In 1889 an
existing windmill was acquired by William Jones, a builder who in fact erected
many properties in Liverpool, but the mill was damaged shortly after purchase
and ceased working. By the beginning of the 20th century, Jones had opened
a brickworks nearby and it is suggested that the mill was repaired and used in
connection with the brick-making business. However, a steam engine had been
installed at the works by 1910, and it is most unlikely that the windmill was used
to drive any machinery other than a pump to de-water the clay pits.

An earlier use of wind power to de-water clay pits in Wales occurred at one
of the Machynys Brick Works near Llanelli in 1878, which it was claimed could

lift 250,000 gallons per day. But in this case the pump is thought to have been one of the annular sail-type pumps, mounted on a steel tower. Invented by Henry Chapping in 1838, but not patented until after 1852, this type of pump became a common sight on farms across the country, being used to raise water for agricultural purposes.

As soon as a pit was dug into the impervious clay, inevitably the pit would quickly fill with water and it was to solve this problem that water power proved to be of practical benefit to brick-makers. In East Yorkshire and Lincolnshire numerous small pumping mills, both tower mills and open trestle hollow post mills, were used to power pumps. A post mill version which existed at Broomfleet Brickworks, to the west of Hull, comprised a wooden pyramid, about nine feet square at the base and about fifteen feet high. Some six feet above ground level was a stage about eighteen inches wide, accessed by a ladder. Cross braces held the upright post in position, the post being a little over a foot in diameter and 17 feet tall. About two-thirds of the way up its length, the post was supported by the top of the pyramid. The cap was essentially two platforms with a skeletal frame, mounted on the post by way of a central hole in each platform. The cap was winded by a vane.

The tower mill version comprised a battered brick tower, some 21 feet high and nine feet in diameter at the base, with a stage at about eight feet above ground level. The tower usually had no cap, the cap framework which carried the windshaft being open to the elements. As with the post mill version, it was winded by a vane.

The technology was the same in both types. The wrought iron wind shaft was cranked, to which crank the pump rod was connected by a wrought iron linkage. The surviving pumps are the simple lift type similar to the cylindrical village pump, with a stroke of 14 inches. The windshaft had a small brake wheel working on the contracting band principle.

The sails varied; some (probably the majority) had common sails but spring sails were also used.

Examples of the tower version have survived at Claxton, Elvington and North Howden in East Yorkshire and at Sutton on Sea in Lincolnshire. An example of the hollow post mill version, which came from the Newport brickworks, is at the Murton Farming Museum near York, awaiting restoration. It is more than likely that examples of this use of wind power occurred in other parts of the country.

Fuller's Earth

As we have seen, towards the end of the 19th century, the ubiquitous steel wind pump began to appear, which was adopted particularly for agricultural purposes. These wind engines, with a wind rose rather than the usual sails, are usually regarded as low-power output engines, which surviving examples generally are. But this has not always been the case. By 1900 some quite large models had appeared (the largest claiming to produce 40hp in an 18mph wind), manufactured by both English and American companies. One such was erected at Odd Down, a few miles to the south of Bath, where it was used to drive machinery at a mine producing fuller's earth.

Fuller's earth has been used for centuries in connection with the treatment of woollen and other cloth but in recent times it has had a wide variety of other uses. The material is in fact a clay, which is only found in commercial quantities in Surrey and at Odd Down, the latter deposit occurring below the layers of Bath stone from where it is extracted by mining.

To render the material usable, it was first necessary to reduce the water content, which was achieved using a rotary kiln. It was then crushed using a Johnson Dragon roller and finally sieved using silk screens. The plant at Odd Down was built *c.*1890 by the Fuller's Earth Union, an amalgamation of small operators who hitherto had operated in competition with each other. Two sources of power were used: a small steam engine to haul trucks up an inclined plane and a wind engine to drive the roller mill and screens. The latter comprised a Halladay wind engine erected on a rectangular wooden frame. The sails had a diameter of 36 feet, with 20 arms and winded by a combination of wind vane and fantail. The tower was a rectangular timber boarded structure, which would have been built by the site owners. The engine was claimed to produce 12hp in an 18mph wind.

Unfortunately the engine came to an untimely end, being destroyed by fire in 1904.

6

Processing Organic Materials

Snuff

Although cigarettes have only been manufactured since the second half of the 19th century, tobacco has been used since Elizabethan times. Up to about 1700, tobacco was smoked as cigars or in clay pipes, but that champion of the gentleman of fashion, Beau Nash, regarded pipe smoking as provincial and commonplace, going so far as to prohibit smoking in the public rooms of Bath. In its place he popularised the taking of snuff. At that date most snuff was imported, but during the 1720s snuff mills began to be established, notably in London, Bristol, Sheffield and Kendal.

As snuff is inhaled through the nose, for obvious practical reasons it has to be ground to a fine powder. Initially snuff was produced by hand, but inevitably a mechanised system evolved using peak edge runner stones to crush the leaves in large shallow elm bowls, the stones, about four feet in diameter, being on a fixed axle and the bowl which held the leaves being rotated. A more sophisticated system was used at a water-powered mill in Morden, where the leaves were placed in an elm mortar, seven-and-a-half inches wide by about fourteen inches deep, with the top few inches widening out. A vertical pestle rolled around the inside to crush the leaves and, as the crushing progressed, the finer powder came to the top and could be lifted off. This arrangement was improved at some stage; the mortar, again made of elm or other hard wood, was shaped as an inverted cone with the tip being rounded into a small dome. An iron pestle, the lower end of which was domed to match the bottom of the mortar, was rolled around the inside of the inverted cone. In some cases the pestles would be arranged around a spur wheel from which a shaft holding the pestle would be driven by a small pinion. But in the larger mills the mortars were probably arranged in banks and driven by a layshaft. In one case at least (Helsington water-powered snuff mill near Kendal) the initial crushing was carried out in a ball mill – a horizontal cylinder in which the leaves were placed together with a number of steel balls (about six inches in diameter). This had the added advantage of thoroughly mixing any flavouring which had been added to the leaves. The crushed material was then sieved, the throughs being ready for sale, but the material left on the sieve was given a further crushing using the inverted conical mortar described above. All of these mechanised systems needed power.

The earliest reference to a wind-powered snuff mill occurs at Devizes in Wiltshire, where two mills were in existence by 1716, but built to crush rape seed. A drawing by William Stukely, dated 1723, shows the two mills as cylindrical towers, with a domed cap and four sails, but a later plan, dated 1759, shows one of them with six sails. In the 1730s several water mills and these two windmills were converted to grind snuff, no doubt to take particular advantage of the market in the nearby town of Bath. By 1784, the premises were occupied by William Laidlow, but in that year he decided to transfer his business to Bristol to be nearer the source of the raw materials. After his departure, the use of the mills changed yet again, this time to corn milling. However, in 1840 one mill was demolished and the other, heavily altered, was incorporated into a Victorian castle and used as a private residence.

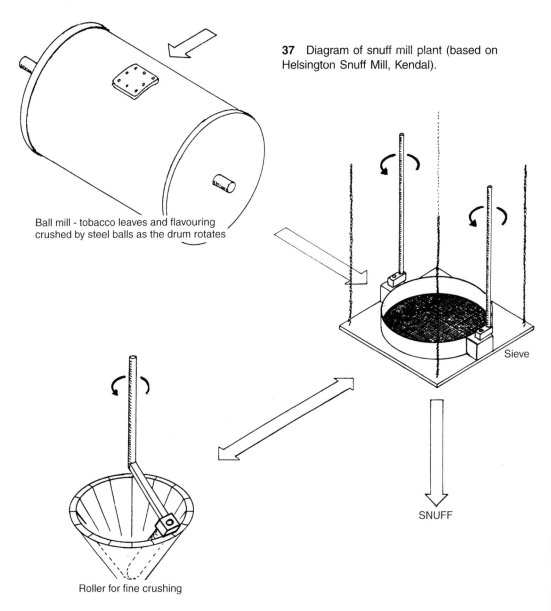

37 Diagram of snuff mill plant (based on Helsington Snuff Mill, Kendal).

Ball mill - tobacco leaves and flavouring crushed by steel balls as the drum rotates

Sieve

SNUFF

Roller for fine crushing

Bristol was a major port for trade with the New World, particularly the importation of tobacco from the plantations around Chesapeake Bay in Virginia. Martin Bodman has identified some 12 snuff mills which operated in Bristol during the 18th century with a further four reputed sites. Of these, nine were water-powered, one had plant powered by both wind and water, and two were solely wind-powered. However, it seems that only five of these mills were purpose-built; the majority were converted from existing mills, mainly grist mills but in one case a fulling mill, a practice which by the 1750s was causing some concern to the local authorities. The trade eventually came to an end during the American War of Independence.

The first wind-powered snuff mill was at Cotham, built as a corn mill in 1725 and converted to snuff milling in 1754. It continued in use until 1776 and by 1807 had been converted to an observatory. It was described as a tall mill and in c.1757 contained 11 snuff mortars.

The second snuff mill to use wind power was the combined wind and water mill known as Locks Mill. There were 20 snuff mills in the water mill and eight in the windmill but each also had two pairs of French millstones and bolting machinery, which may indicate that the complex was originally built as a corn mill. The windmill was a tower built of stone.

The third snuff mill stood on Clifton Down, built as a corn mill in 1767 (at a cost of £300). It was subsequently converted to snuff milling but was short-lived, being burnt down in 1777 and later rebuilt as an observatory, which still stands.

In addition to the above, there is evidence to suggest that other windmills were used to grind snuff around Bristol. One seems likely to have stood at Kings Weston Down, with a further two possibly at Barrow Gurney.

Bristol was an interesting town for power sources, having both suitable water power and wind power sites. Unfortunately, there was also a demand for power from other industries, so that, to find water-powered sites, the snuff millers had to go some three or four miles outside the town. The nearest water-powered snuff mills to the town centre were at Redland, which in its early life had water supply problems, and Locks Mill, which worked in conjunction with a windmill. In fact, the two snuff mills closest to the city centre (and, therefore, the market and the docks) were the windmills at Clifton Down and Cotham.

Although the main snuff producing centres were the towns mentioned earlier, snuff mills did appear in other places. Over in Norwich, an interesting snuff mill appeared at Carrow Hill in the early 1780s, being built inside one of the old towers which formed part of the medieval town wall and which had been leased out for commercial purposes once their defensive function had ended. On top of the tower, a ten-sided smock with a domed cap, four sails and winding wheel was erected. There were no windows in the smock and it appears likely that the drive was taken down to the machinery housed in the old tower. Snuff milling came to an end around 1800.

The last wind-powered snuff mill operated at Wigton in Cumbria, not far from the port of Whitehaven where tobacco was also imported. A stone tower

38 Black Tower Snuff Mill, Norwich. The tower was originally part of the town's defences but, when this use became redundant, the Town Council leased it for commercial purposes. In about 1782 the windmill was added to grind snuff (the plant probably being located in the stone tower below the mill) and was later for a short period used to drive cotton spinning machines.

mill, originally built to grind corn, it was converted to snuff milling in the 19th century and continued in operation until *c*.1840. In this case a ready market may have been found amongst the miners working in the local coal pits, snuff being an acceptable alternative to pipe smoking down a coal mine.

Rope making and Scutching

The traditional material for making ropes was the fibrous part of the hemp plant. To extract the fibres, the plant was first soaked in water to rot away the core of the plant (retting) and then beaten to separate the fibre from the stalk.

The beating could be carried out in one of two ways. The older method simply used stampers, a process called bawling. A later system, known as scutching, involved the use of a rimless wheel, where the spokes were slats of wood set at an angle to the shaft, like the blades of a fan. The wheel was rotated and the stalks presented to it manually in bundles.

Once the fibre had been separated from the unwanted parts of the plant, it was spun to produce a yarn; two yarns were then twisted together to make a length of twine. To make a rope, a frame called a jack was used, which had three hooks set as at the three corners of a triangle, connected by a gear wheel or pulley wire to a handle, so that, when the handle was turned, the hooks spun round individually. A number of twines were tied to each hook, the number dependent upon the thickness of the rope required, and the other ends were fixed to a single freely swivelling hook, mounted on a frame called a sledge. The rope maker's assistant turned the handle, causing the twines to twist, and the rope maker, standing by the sledge, held the three bunches of twines apart with a grooved wooden top, to prevent the twines becoming tangled. Once the twines were sufficiently twisted, the rope maker walked towards the jack, keeping the top between the three strands, and the rope simply twisted into shape behind him. The rope had to be kept in a straight line whilst the process was undertaken, which required a long narrow pathway, given the name 'rope walk'. In later years these were often covered over and maps of many towns show these distinctive long and narrow buildings.

The bawling or scutching of the hemp was the part of the process which required power.

Ropes were in particular demand in the days of sailing ships, from small sailing vessels, to clippers voyaging to distant shores, and to the navy defending the country's trading interests. The Admiralty had a number of rope making concerns in the Bridport area, all using water power. But at nearby Poole, in 1784, one Lawrence Tullock established a twine spinning business, probably for use in making fishing nets. He established his premises on land reclaimed from the mud flats, known as West Butts Green. By 1791 he had built a 'timber windmill' for bawling hemp, clearly a small smock mill. All the other tower windmills in Dorset were built of stone and it seems likely that he chose to build the mill of timber because it was built on reclaimed mud, which would not have been sufficiently consolidated to take the weight of a stone structure. The mill continued in use until 1840.

In addition to maritime uses, rope had many applications in agriculture, and also in mining, to haul kibbles and, later, cages up mine shafts. Such ropes were in demand in Shropshire for the lead mines and collieries in the county. By the start of the 19th century a rope works had been established at the top of Lyth Hill, near Shrewsbury, to meet this demand. The siting seems to have been carefully chosen, as Colin Breeze recalls his father (who worked at the ropery as a very young man) telling him:

> The rope-walk itself was of tremendous length. It stretched from the top of the hill to what was known as the first gate in the Bayston direction, for something over half a mile … . The rope maker, with a huge bundle of hemp around his waist would leave the wheel turner at the top of the hill and slowly walk away and vanish out of site in making the long ropes … Turning the wheel as I did, the rope maker at the other end of the yarn was out of my site [*sic*].

39 Lyth Hill Ropery near Shrewsbury, built *c*.1835.

The output at Lyth Hill was not limited to long ropes for mines. The firm's ledger includes sales of bell ropes, a range of agricultural ropes and ordinary twine, with customers ranging across a wide area around Shrewsbury.

In 1835 a windmill was built for use by the rope maker, which comprised a small brick tower, about thirty feet to the curb, with a typical West Midlands cap, four sails (two commons and two springs) and winding wheel. The internal machinery is not recorded but it was most likely rotating scutching blades. Having said that, a rope half a mile long would be extremely heavy and the question arises as to whether wind power might also have been used to drive the jack? The windmill continued in operation until the early 20th century and the empty tower still stands, in a private garden.

The bawling and scutching mills mentioned so far were used specifically in conjunction with rope making, but many such mills simply prepared the hemp or flax for textile purposes. The remains of a small tower mill at Stoneykirk, Wigtownshire, thought to have been used to scutch flax, comprise a small cylindrical tower of rubble stone, some 10ft 6ins in height and 12 feet in diameter. The low height of the mill suggests that it is in fact the roundhouse of a former post mill, but it seems more likely that it was originally a taller structure, now reduced in height.

Textiles

The mention of textile mills undoubtedly calls to mind the dark satanic mills of legend, almost the antithesis of the romantic windmill. Nevertheless, there have been attempts to use wind power in connection with aspects of textile manufacture. Yorkshire, the home of the woollen trade, was able to make use of water power until the 20th century, although the availability of steam power enabled some quite colossal mills to be built in the West Riding. But the West

Riding is extremely hilly and provides sites suitable for the windmill. One such was Morley, where in 1787 a windmill, built some years earlier as a corn mill, was adapted to drive a scribbling machine, a device which carded the wool into slivers ready for spinning. It is not clear how long the venture survived. The mill was still in existence in 1841, but by that date had reverted to corn milling.

The cotton industry was concentrated to the west of the Pennines in Lancashire, and it should be mentioned that one writer has claimed that a cotton mill at Preston built in 1777 was powered by a windmill. However, Don Paterson has pointed out that a steam-powered cotton mill and a wind-powered corn mill existed in Moor Lane, on one site and having the same owner, so this claim is doubtful.

There was a short-lived cotton mill in Norwich. An advertisement in the *Norfolk Chronicle* of May 1800 offers for immediate rental: '. . a tower windmill lately used in the manufacture of cotton, with the tower on which the mill is situate and an extensive range of offices lately used as spinning rooms.' In fact these are the premises in which the snuff mill operated, mentioned above, in which case it can only have been converted in the 1790s and it does not seem to have continued after the 1800 advertisement. By 1833 the mill had disappeared and, when the old tower was struck by a thunderstorm, the press report states that the upper room was occupied by 'a society of artisans assembled for astronomical observations'.

The small town of Diss in Norfolk had a total of nine windmills, a mixture of post, tower and smock mills. One of these, a post mill in Victoria Road, was being used in 1826 to 'set in motion' a factory for spinning coarse yarns. Unfortunately, nothing else seems to be known about this mill, which may be the only windmill which directly drove spinning frames with any degree of success.

There was one other windmill used to drive a cotton mill, but in this case only indirectly, built by the Unwin family at Sutton-in-Ashfield in Nottinghamshire and described as the first mill or factory to be built in the town. Dating from the 1770s,

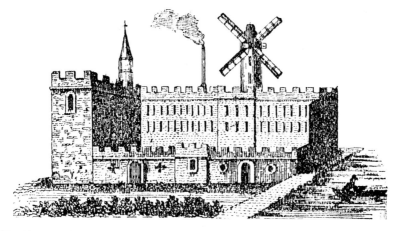

40 Unwin's Cotton Mill, Sutton in Ashfield, Nottinghamshire, built in the 1770s.

the factory was a glorious piece of Tudor revival architecture, three storeys high and built of local stone. Sutton is located on the eastern slopes of the Pennines, in the Nottinghamshire coalfield and, as the site is on the watershed between the River Maun running eastwards and the River Erewash running westwards, Unwin must have recognised that he did not have adequate water power available to drive the factory, even with the aid of a large mill pond. The mill stands on the River Maun, very close to its source. Consequently he included a windmill in his factory complex to pump water back from the tail race into the mill pond, another example of a water-returning engine. The windmill was a tall cylindrical tower, probably some 60 feet to the curb, of local stone and with four patent sails (eventually). Sometime after 1810, a steam engine was added and for a number of years the mill had available the three sources of power. Interestingly, the town had a mixture of wind and water mills. Below Unwin's mill several mill ponds survive, one of which provided power for a grain mill, but the town also had two windmills; one built in the 1810s was another extremely tall tower mill, standing some 70 feet to the curb and fitted with six sails.

Oak bark
Cattle must surely have been the most useful animals known to man down the centuries. There is very little of the animal which does not supply one of his needs; even the horns had a number of uses, as drinking vessels, to carry his musket powder into battle and even a basic musical instrument. The part with which we are concerned here is the skin or, more properly in the case of cattle, the hide. When converted into leather, this had a multitude of domestic and industrial uses.

The conversion of hide to leather involved, firstly, removal of the hair and other organic matter, which was achieved by soaking the hide in a lime pit, then scraping off by hand the unwanted material. Secondly, the hides would be tanned, i.e. soaked in a liquor containing tannin, the central part of the process which effected the conversion. Thirdly, a range of different finishing processes applied, which vary dependent upon the use to which the leather was to be put, e.g. shoe soles, harness, fancy goods, furniture, clothing etc. The most widely used material to produce the tanning liquor was oak bark, although by the mid-19th century it was becoming increasingly difficult to obtain adequate supplies from indigenous sources.

Tanneries were very widely spread. There can be few if any market towns which have not had at least one tannery during most of their history. Until the mid-19th century the process was entirely manual, apart from the crushing of the bark, which had been done originally by horse mill. Bark does not require crushing to a very fine powder and it was realised at some stage that ordinary mill stones could be used for the purpose. The stones would be set wider apart than when used for grain milling and it is possible that the runner stone may have had a fixed rhynd to produce a degree of consistency, rather than the floating arrangement more usual in grain mills.

The earliest examples of which there are any remains occurred in north-west Cumbria, two dating from the 18th century and one from *c.*1829. They were all tower mills, one of which, at Wigton, is of particular interest. It is built of uncoursed red sandstone and, in 1810, contained one pair of French stones, one pair of grey stones, a barley mill and cylinders, and a bark mill. It is not clear what is meant by a 'bark mill' here but it would appear to be something different from the millstones and may have been the type of bark mill illustrated by Pyne (*Delineation of the Arts, Crafts, Manufactures etc. of Great Britain*), namely a single edge runner stone, the rim of which has been serrated.

The tower was some 55 feet high, with four single-sided sails, and had an unusual feature in that it was not cylindrical in plan. A survey carried out by the eminent Cumbrian historian, Michael Davies-Shiel, shows that the external dimensions at ground level were 37 feet on its east-west axis and 35 feet on its north-south axis. Neither was the batter symmetrical, the batter being greater on the eastern side than on the western. Davies-Shiel suggests that this may indicate that the mill had a fixed cap, with the sails facing westwards, the eastern side of the tower acting like a buttress to counteract the pressure. If this mill did have a fixed cap it would be unique in English mill technology.

The mill stood on low ground, amidst open fields to the north of the town, a location which may have contributed to its undoing. In 1843 the stretch of the Maryport and Carlisle railway was opened to Wigton, the line running along an

41 Tower of Bark Mill at Wigton, Cumbria, built *c.*1790. The photograph is taken from the footbridge between the platforms at the adjacent railway station. When first built, the station had a large block of station buildings, where the notice board and the 'bus' shelter now stand, which would have very seriously interfered with the flow of air to the windmill sails. Not surprisingly, the use of wind power ceased shortly after the railway was built in 1843.

embankment across the low ground on which the mill had been built. The Wigton station was built on top of the embankment a few yards to the west of the mill. Regardless of whether or not the windmill was unidirectional, i.e. having a fixed cap, the rather imposing station buildings on top of the embankment would have seriously impeded the predominant wind flow. Consequently, shortly afterwards, the sails were removed and a steam engine installed. As some compensation, the adjacent railway provided a cheap source of coal.

Moving into the 19th century, we find several bark mills in the eastern counties. In East Yorkshire a corn mill at Beverley was engulfed by the expansion of an adjoining tannery in 1826 and used for bark crushing for a few years. This tannery provided leather for the usual range of products but they had a particularly good trade in making leather straps for the flying shuttle on textile looms. In the 1980s, an archaeological dig in the centre of Beverley unearthed a six-foot diameter millstone, with a very large central eye – something like a large polo mint. It is thought this may have been used to crush bark at an earlier horse-powered bark mill. At Market Weighton, a tan yard was advertised for sale in 1852, having 91 tan pits, a wind bark mill and a horse bark mill.

In Lincolnshire, a large tannery concern, including a windmill for grinding bark at St Peter's-at-Gowts, was advertised in 1819. At Louth we hear that a windmill was destroyed by fire in 1857, which had been used as a bark mill since 1840 at least.

In East Anglia, a tannery in Heigham Street, Norwich, had a wind bark mill by 1836, which continued in use until 1863. Although the windmill was demolished in that year, the tannery continued in operation until 1908. Another at Streetley End in Cambridgeshire, built as a corn mill in 1802, was converted to crush bark two years later, for an adjoining tannery.

An interesting bark mill operated at Sprowston in Norfolk. Built by 1826, it comprised a brick tower mill with four patent sails. The plant comprised two pairs of French stones, flour mill and jumper, stripping machine etc. It is not difficult to interpret the 'stripping machine' as a device for removing bark from a log. Two later advertisements, both dated 11 December 1858, may throw some light on the matter. The first offers for sale 'a pair of cones for grinding bark, greaves, oil cake etc.'. The second offers to let 'a brick tower windmill driving two pairs of stones, flour mill & jumper'. The inference from these three advertisements taken together is that, firstly, the 'stripping machine' was a unit containing the pair of cones and, secondly, that the mill was built as a corn mill, with either when built or added later, an auxiliary item of plant, incorporating a pair of cone-shaped edge runners, which could be used for a number of purposes, including grinding bark. (Greaves are the fibrous matter or skin found in animal fat which forms a sediment in melting and is pressed into cakes for dog food, fish bait etc.)

Two more windmills were used to crush bark in England: at Wantage, a post mill, and at Wellington in Somerset.

One final example is known, at Llanbadarn Fawr near Aberystwyth, an area which was well served by water mills. By 1834 a mill had been built which

42 Llanbadarn Bark Mill, built in the early 19th century. It is believed that the mill had a fantail. Drawing by T. Hastings.

is shown in a sketch made in 1849 by T. Hastings (*The Old Windmill and Church at Llanbadarn near Aberystwyth*). It shows a stone tower mill, with five sails and an ogee cap. This type of cap is most unusual in Wales, as is the use of five sails, and there must have been some outside influence involved in the millwrighting, either through the tanners or more likely through a millwright who had travelled widely.

Bones

Another part of the animal put to good use was its bones, when towards the end of the 18th century it was discovered that bone meal had a value as a dressing on agricultural land. The bones were crushed using fairly simple machines, comprising a pair of cast-iron toothed rollers. Power was needed to drive the rollers.

43 Southwark Bone Mill, built in the 1790s on top of a former meeting house.

A few windmills had bone crushers, the earliest being a rather interesting mill built at Southwark in London around 1790. Here we have another example of the space problem in the capital. The mill comprised a hollow post mill located on top of a three-storey circular building which had been erected as a meeting house. In addition to crushing bones, it also ground corn, paint and gypsum.

At Scarborough, a corn mill built around 1820 was converted entirely to bone crushing in 1828, a use which continued until 1840. In Lincolnshire, a saw mill at Scawby also had a bone crusher.

Drugs for medicinal purposes

The 18th-century apothecary used a wide range of materials for the production of 'specifics'. These would be materials of both organic and inorganic origin, many of which would need to be ground into powder form, in most cases by hand, using a mortar and pestle. However, there are two cases where wind power may have been used to relieve some of the hard work.

The first stood at Lambeth, in London. In 1873, a writer claimed that this mill had at one time belonged to the Apothecaries' Company and was used by them for grinding and pounding their drugs. This claim was adopted by subsequent

44   Lambeth Drugs Mill before 1759. Aquatint by Paul Sandby.

writers although no reference appeared relating to this mill in the Company's papers. Michael Short has sifted through the available evidence in some detail and has discovered that the mill was used by a druggist called George Rutt from 1759 until his death in 1778. Interestingly, it appears that the mill was not built originally for this purpose, as an advertisement in 1730, which is thought to relate to this mill, describes it as a potter's windmill.

We do not have any indication of the plant employed in the mill, but we do know about its external appearance from two views by the eminent watercolourist, Paul Sandby. The mill is shown as a brick tower, some 35 feet to the curb, with a wide braced stage at about fifteen feet above ground level, fitted with four common sails and winded by chain wheel. The sails were of very light construction and braced with tie rods between the tips to prevent undue whip. They were also held by guy ropes to a bowsprit extending from the end of the windshaft, to give further stiffness. But interpretation of the cap is a problem. It is shown as an eight-sided truncated pyramid, surmounted by a small shed-like structure, with the windshaft entering the cap at about what may be called the floor level of the shed. An attempt to scale the 'shed' off the picture gives the external width as about six feet, which at best would only allow space for a brakewheel of about four feet diameter.

The other drug mill stood at the New Barracks on Woodbridge Road, Ipswich and, according to the *Ipswich Journal* of 1804, it comprised a small windmill for producing drugs using iron cylinders. This, and a nearby post mill, were situated within the barracks, which were built to house soldiers at a time when the Napoleonic invasion was feared. Both mills had disappeared by 1812.

Others

Two one-off uses should be mentioned for the sake of completeness.

The first is a small smock mill with four common sails which was built at King's Lynn across the Caywood river from St Ann's Fort c.1681, which produced starch. The sale of coarse linen by Lynn men was long established in the town and the starch was probably sold to the linen weavers for stiffening the linen. It seems likely that the starch was produced from locally grown wheat.

The second was Willis' Mill which stood in Ordnance Place, Chatham. Again, a smock mill, for grinding corn and spices (pepper, ginger etc.), which was no doubt sited for the convenience of handling imported materials. The mill continued in operation until c.1875.

7

Brass Making, Mines and Quarries

Brass making

Brass is an alloy of copper and zinc, a malleable material, which, at the start of the 18th century, was used for the production of wire and battery ware. Wire was in demand to produce pins for carding wool prior to spinning. Battery ware, so called because it was hammered out of sheets of brass (and indeed tin and copper), comprised pots and pans of various sizes for both industrial and domestic use.

Although some brass was produced in England before 1700, most was imported from Germany and Holland, and the conversion into finished articles was achieved by beating brass sheet manually into the required shape. An early mill flourished at Esher in Surrey which manufactured brass wire but it was in Bristol that the British brass industry started to develop. By 1700, Bristol was a thriving commercial centre and large port, second only to London. Copper ore was transported by sea from the Cornish mines, the zinc ore calamine had been discovered in the Mendips, and ample supplies of coal were available in the Somerset coal fields. (It is sometimes overlooked that the availability of coal was of prime importance to industry long before the advent of the steam engine.)

The most important of the early Bristol brass making concerns was started by Abraham Darby, later to make his name as the first person to smelt cast iron using coke. He started the production of brass around 1702 and, shortly after that date, established the Baptist Mills on the River Frome, his company generally being known as the Bristol Brass Company. Angerstein visited Bristol in 1754 and took considerable interest in the various manufacturing concerns, particularly those dealing with metal working. He records what he found at the Baptist Mills brass works, his entry being followed by another headed Calamine Roasting and Milling, which ends, 'Here are two mills for grinding calamine, driven by water. A windmill of brick was also being built for this purpose, because the grinding is slow'.

This slowness probably arose from what has been described as the 'fluctuating River Frome'. For details of the construction of the windmill, in the British Library there is a picture by Grimm entitled *A View of a Brass Works near Bristol* which shows a tall tower mill, the body of which is almost cylindrical, fitted with four double common sails supported by a bowsprit and with tie rods linking each sails at its outer end. General opinion is that this is the mill at the Baptist Works. From Coulthard and Watts (*Windmills of Somerset*) it is clear that the mill depicted by

Grimm is very much in line with millwrighting practice in the area at that date. Early mills in Somerset were, of course, post mills but from about 1730 onwards many of them were replaced by tower mills. The surviving Ashton Windmill at Chapel Allerton, possibly built as early as 1736, is a prime example.

After Darby's departure to Coalbrookdale (c.1709), the Baptist Mills were run by Nehemiah Champion, who made significant improvements in the method of production. His two sons, John and William, joined him in the firm and also took a great interest in improving techniques. It is surprising that, up to this point, although it was known that copper and calamine could be alloyed to form brass, it was not realised that the calamine was in fact zinc carbonate, and it was the zinc content that formed the alloy. Failure to appreciate this had resulted in a considerable waste of calamine (and zinc) as zinc vaporises at a comparatively low temperature; consequently some of the available zinc was literally disappearing into thin air. Whilst touring Europe to learn about foreign methods, William met several metallurgists who were beginning to make this connection and on his return to Baptist Mills he set to work on this discovery, eventually working out the first large-scale process for the commercial production of metallic zinc, which he patented in 1738.

To exploit his patent, William formed a new company in 1746 and decided to build an entirely new brass factory, and in doing so he took an entirely different approach. The old brass company had been very fragmented. It had bought copper from smelters in the town, it had made brass at Baptist Mills, but the finishing had been carried out at various locations on the River Avon and its tributaries. At least three of the battery works were former water-powered fulling mills which had been taken over and converted by the company. William Champion's new factory, which he built at Warmley, was designed to enable the entire process of copper and brass manufacture to be carried out on one site, from the smelting of the copper and calamine ores to the production of finished articles: wire, pins and domestic wares.

A factory of this size needed considerable power and Champion installed two water wheels which were fed from a 13-acre pond formed by impounding water from the Warmley Brook. This proved inadequate, so in 1748 a steam engine with a 36-inch cylinder was installed, to lift water back from the tail race into the millpond, in effect a water-returning engine. This also proved inadequate, so in 1749 it was replaced by a 48-inch cylinder steam engine. This was still inadequate, so in 1761 it was in turn replaced by a cylinder of over 72 inches diameter. The engine was required to lift the water some 18 feet and it is claimed that the second engine could raise 189,000 gallons of water per hour. If this is correct, the rating of the engine would have been about 17hp and, assuming that the length and number of strokes remained constant, the third engine would be rated at about 39hp.

Champion also erected two horse gins and a windmill at the factory but there is some uncertainty as to when the windmill was built and what it was used for. It certainly existed in 1760 but it is not mentioned by Angerstein following his

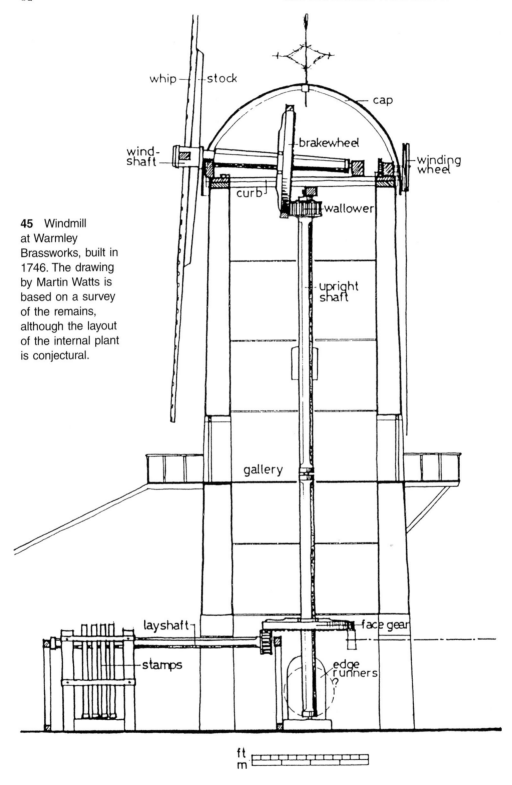

45 Windmill at Warmley Brassworks, built in 1746. The drawing by Martin Watts is based on a survey of the remains, although the layout of the internal plant is conjectural.

visit in 1754. A visitor in 1760 (another Swedish spy) reported that it was used to pump water from the tail race back into the mill pond. But a year later, an inventory of the company's premises contained the following entry: 'One windmill with stamps etc. ...'

It is not clear how close to the well-guarded premises the two Swedish visitors got, although it must be unlikely that Angerstein would fail to have seen a windmill. It is quite likely that Champion deliberately misled the other. However, applying the evidence we have available, a possible scenario might be as follows:

1746   Factory built with two waterwheels
1748   Steam engine with 36" cylinder added
1749   Cylinder replaced by one of 48" (possibly 17hp)
1754/60   Windmill added to pump water (see below *)
1761   Cylinder replaced by one of 72" (possibly 39hp) and windmill converted
            to ore stamping

(* One might expect a mill with common sails of this size to produce something in the region of 10/15hp, although, having regard to the fact that the gears would have been the simple trundle and lantern pinion arrangement, it is likely to be nearer the lower figure.)

Either way, what is certain is that Champion installed a windmill in his factory before 1761 which was used to crush ore and possibly to pump water.

The empty tower still stands today. It is built of coursed sandstone, some 60 feet to the curb, with an internal diameter at the base of 16 feet. At ground level there are four large openings set at each quadrant. When operational it would have been fitted with four common sails and winded by chain wheel. The internal floor area is rather small, so it is likely that a drive or drives were taken through these openings by line shaft into an adjoining building, where the stamps would have been located.

The selection of this site by Champion, with its unsatisfactory supply of water, shows how difficult it was even as early as 1746 to find a suitable water power site on the rivers around Bristol. By 1746 the best sites were already occupied, several by the old Bristol Company, Saltford Mill, which still survives, being a good example. In 1761 Champion was trying to expand the business and, to do so, he constructed a new copper smelting works at Kingswood, some two miles away from the Warmley factory, but on a site where no water power was available. The new premises comprised 17 furnaces and were referred to by Champion as his Upper Works, but by the time the Tithe map was published in 1844 the factory was generally known as the Cupola (cupola being the local name for a copper smelting furnace). This factory would only need power to drive the ore crushing stamps and it has been suggested by A. Braine (*History of Kingswood Forest*) that a 55-foot high tower which stood near the site was a windmill used for this purpose. He states that in the basement of the tower there was a circular room, 18 feet in diameter with walls four feet thick. This does not sound like a windmill – if it was anything to do with the smelting works, it was more likely to have been a furnace of some sort.

46 Brassworks and windmill near Bristol, built *c.*1754. Detail from a drawing by H. Grimm, 1788.

Brass was also manufactured in other parts of the country. We have already mentioned Esher, but this factory was taken over by the old Bristol company and seems to have gone out of use fairly early on. Another location was Macclesfield in Cheshire where Charles Roe, hitherto involved in the silk industry, decided to divert into the production of copper and brass. In 1758 he built a smelting works, using copper ore from the mines at Alderley Edge, some six miles away. Coal for the furnaces was readily available, but calamine had to be shipped up the River Weaver to Northwich, 20 miles by road from Macclesfield. Some finishing was carried out at the works but in 1763 and 1766 Roe opened mills on the River Dane where he produced sheet, wire and battery wares, using water power. Roe had three large reservoirs near the smelting works but he needed this for use in the production process. Consequently, to crush the ores he erected a windmill, probably using stampers, which is shown in an early 19th-century engraving to be a small tower mill with four common sails and a domed cap.

As the mines at Alderley Edge were worked out, Row became a leader in the exploitation of the enormous copper mine at Parys Mountain in Anglesey. Macclesfield was obviously poorly sited in relation to this new source of ore and the company eventually transferred its operations to South Wales (where wages were cheaper). In 1801 the Macclesfield Brass Works closed down, at which stage the windmill was converted to grain milling. There is no trace of the windmill today but it is pleasing to note that it stood in what is now called Windmill Lane at the junction with Calamine Street, just across the road from Copper Lane.

Mines and Quarries

Dealing first with coal mining, one normally associates this with the Newcomen engine, the first of which was installed at a coal mine in Dudley in 1712. Indeed, there are very few references to wind power being used to de-water coal mines. But the few that do exist indicate that such power may have been used, or at least tried, more than is generally realised.

In relation to William Champion's company, it was mentioned above that in 1761 he erected new copper smelting furnaces at Kingswood. At the same time he entered into agreements with the local colliery owners for the purchase of coal. Joan Day explains that this encouraged the colliers to improve output, and some of them installed horse whims and windmills to enable them to increase production. The horse mills would have been used for winding and the windmills for pumping water out of the mines. These improvements did in fact lead to an increase in output, which caused a problem for Champion, resulting in overstocking of coal. The use of wind-powered pumps to de-water coal mines was not new in Somerset at this date, as one had been built at Wraxall in 1701 to raise water from a depth of 12 fathoms.

Another interesting account of the use of wind power at coal mines is given by John Farey:

> In the year 1708, a plan was projected in Scotland, for drawing water from coal mines by windmills and pumps, but there was at that time no person in Scotland capable of executing the work, except John Young, the millwright of Montrose, who had been sent at the expense of that town to Holland, to inspect the mills in use there. It was suggested, that if this millwright could not be procured, application should be made to the mechanical priest in Lancashire for his advice. Windmills were accordingly erected at several collieries; but although they were efficient machines at certain times, they were very irregular; and in a long period of calm weather, the mines would be drowned, and all the workmen thrown idle. The contingent expenses were also very great and they were only applicable in open and elevated situations.

Farey goes on to say that in 1709, John, Earl of Mar, sent his manager to Newcastle to inspect machinery used in that area. The engineer reported that the machines in use there were water wheels and horse engines, with chain pumps, the pits being between 120 and 180 feet deep, with a few as deep as 360 feet. Chain pumps had been used to de-water mines in Eastern Europe as far back as the 14th century, two versions being known, the bucket-and-chain and the rag-and-chain, which are well recorded by Ramelli and others. (The bucket and chain pump must not be confused with the bucket pump, i.e. the typical village pump, used to de-water clay pits.)

Duckham (*A History of the Scottish Coal Industry*) points out that there was doubt about the value of wind power in Scotland due to the lack of wind, which he suggests is rather surprising. It was recognised, however, that pumping by wind would be sufficient for a pit of moderate depth and, for smaller pits relying on local sales, a Newcomen engine was a luxury which could not be afforded.

We know of several Scottish mines which used wind power to drive pumps. Four were in the area of the Firth of Forth, the first being built by John and Alexander Landale in 1732 at a pit leased from the 5th Earl of Leven at Balgonie. In fact, both wind and water power were used, the windmill driving eight-inch pumps which raised water from a depth of 14 fathoms. Unfortunately, the mine was not able to compete with a nearby colliery at Balbinnim and was laid up in 1743. The second was built at Strathore, to the north of Kirkcaldy, in *c*.1738. An estimate for the erection of the windmill was submitted by Stephen Rowe in the sum of £115, and it is thought the mill raised water from a depth of 30 fathoms. The third windmill was built *c*.1746 on land owned by the Earl of Kellie, which it is claimed, drained the coal adequately. We will return to this mine later in connection with salt works. The fourth, known as Bridgness, was built at Bo'ness and Carridon and dates from *c*.1750. It comprised a cylindrical tower, 42 feet to the curb and 23 feet diameter at the base. It was out of use by the 1850s and in 1915 converted to a dwelling. The top has been corbelled outward and crenellated, and a staircase added in a separate circular structure attached to the tower, producing an overall appearance with more than a strong hint of the Scottish Baronial style!

The final windmill was built in 1737 on the opposite coast, at Westmuir Colliery near Glasgow. It raised water with 'tolerable efficiency' until a windy night in January 1740 when it was destroyed in a gale and never rebuilt, perhaps a surprising end in view of the comments quoted by Duckham.

A drawing of the type of wind pump used at these mines exists amongst the Rothes Manuscripts. It shows a stone tower mill, with four sails mounted on a timber windshaft. The upright shaft (geared up approximately one to two) has a cogged wheel at its lower end which drives a similar wheel (geared down approximately two to one). This driven wheel is fixed on a short horizontal shaft with a crank at each end. Passing through the wall of the mill, a few feet above ground level, are two horizontal beams, pivoted at about the point where they pass through the wall. The inner end of each beam is connected by a tie rod to one of the cranks. The outer end of each beam has an arch head which is located directly over the pumping shaft, each carrying two chains, each chain connected to a lift pump. The lift is carried out in two stages, one chain being attached to the lower pump, the other to the higher. So far as can be judged from the drawing, the throw of each pump is unlikely to be more than about two feet and, assuming the estimation of the gear ratios is correct, the cranked shaft must be rotating at about the same speed as the sails, say 10 or 12 rpm.

Farey does not give any details of the 'mechanical priest of Lancashire' but it may be no coincidence that it was at Wigan, in that county, where Edmund Lee developed and patented his fantail (see page 36). It is hardly likely that Lee (nor Melling) could be the priest referred to in 1708 but it must indicate that wind power was being used in Lancashire at the beginning of the 18th century to de-water coal mines.

As we have seen, Lee's fantail was first applied to two mills in Lancashire, one being Sir Rodger Brock's mine near Wigan, built in the late 1740s. We know it was a tower mill with four sails and that it drove either a bucket pump or a force pump, with the pump rod being operated by a crank at the rear end of the windshaft. The mill had an early form of adjustable sail, which, in the corn mill version, was controlled by means of a striking rod which passed through the windshaft. In the pumping version, installed at the coal mine, the presence of the crank precluded the striking rod from passing all the way through the shaft. To overcome this, the striking rod ended short of the tail, where it was fitted with a number of bars at right angles to the rod, which passed through slots in the windshaft. The bars were attached to an iron ring, in effect forming a wheel, which pressed against an iron-hinged frame connected to the striking weights.

Blake Tyson (*Two Post-mills at Whitehaven*) records an earlier example of wind power being used to de-water a coal mine, in Cumbria. Sir John Lowther opened a coal mine at Whitehaven in the 1680s, which was drained by an adit, but where there were good coal reserves below adit level. It was, therefore, necessary to arrange for a pump to lift water from the lower workings up to the drainage adit. The suggestion that wind power should be used was met with a certain amount of scepticism by Sir John's agent, who wanted to use the tried and tested method of a horse gin. But his lordship was attracted to the idea and set about investigating the possibility. He approached the matter cautiously, making enquiries around the country, particularly in Newcastle where by 1686 several wind-powered pumps

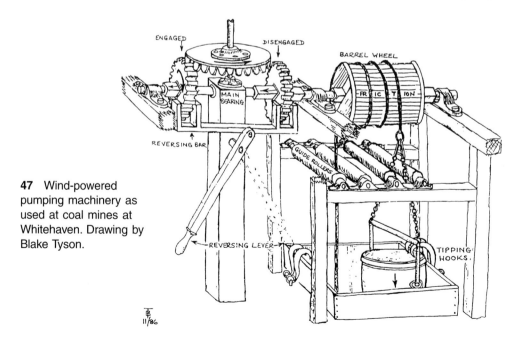

47 Wind-powered pumping machinery as used at coal mines at Whitehaven. Drawing by Blake Tyson.

were in operation. After careful consideration and discussion concerning the design, work was put in hand towards the end of 1686.

The machine doing the pumping was a clever design, possibly the idea of a local engineer called Pelling. The system comprised a horizontal barrel around which a chain was wrapped, with a bucket at each end. Thus, when the barrel was rotated, one bucket was raised, the other was lowered. At the top of the shaft, a hook would catch the rim of the bucket, causing it to tip up and discharge its load. (This device could also be used to raise coal.) There was a drawback to this system, in that it was necessary to reverse the direction in which the barrel rotated once a bucket had discharged, which was achieved by a simple gear system, but had to be operated manually. Although ingenious, such a device can only have raised a small quantity of water per hour.

As the task to be performed in this case was to lift water up to the drainage adit, not the surface, the framework holding the barrel, and the gears, were located underground, at the adit level. To get power down to this level, a wind engine in the form of a hollow post mill was built on the surface, with a vertical spindle which passed down through the post and then the shaft, into the mine below. The length of the shaft is not reported but it is known that it was made at a forge in Ireland. This is probably not a reflection on English forges but an indication of the difficulty of transporting a long length of iron across the hills of the Lake District. A sea journey from Ireland was a much simpler proposition.

Another interesting point to emerge from the correspondence between Sir John and his agent is the number and design of the sails fitted to the mill. The millwright was a gentleman by the name of Satterthwaite, who proposed to fit six sails, each sail to have cloth either side of the main timber. Sir John expressed concern over this, preferring four sails, and suggesting that each sail should be what we today called single-sided, but with a single plank on the leading edge in the 'Dutch fashion'. It appears that the millwright may have got his own way, as J. Hughes (*Cumberland Windmills*) states that a wind engine with six sails was erected by Sir John Lowther at his coal pits at Whitehaven.

So, we know of the use of wind power to pump water out of coal mines in Scotland, Cumbria, Lancashire and Somerset. But the earliest recorded example is found at Wollaton in Nottinghamshire. Richard Smith (*Early Coal-mining around Nottingham 1500-1650*) gives details of horse mills erected at pits in this area. In addition, the accounts show that a windmill was built in 1578, which was to be used to power a chain of buckets. The estimates from the accounts, quoted by Smith, include:

> sawing boards for the windmill …
> 50 yds of canvas for seale clothes for the myll …
> making buckettes for the new mill …
> 2 par of buckettes for the wynd mylle pumps …

It is worth pausing for a moment at this point to speculate on what this mill looked like. The usual form of windmill at this date was still the post mill, a small light structure, with the cross trees buried in the ground to provide stability. (As late as the 1540s a corn post mill of this description was built at Bridlington.) If the base of the post is buried in the ground, the hollow post mill concept cannot apply. It is not until the idea of raising the bottom of the post and cross trees onto piers, so that there is a working space between the bottom of the post and the ground, that the concept of the hollow post mill becomes a possibility. The earliest surviving example we have of a post mill raised on piers, i.e. at Bourn in Cambridgeshire, was still some fifty years into the future.

We know from Agricola's *De Re Metallica* published in 1556, that the windmill was known in connection with mining in Europe and that Sir Francis Willoughby, the owner of the mine at Wollaton, had a translation of part of this work, but only that dealing with suction pumps. One of Agricola's illustrations shows a rectangular box mounted over a mine shaft, containing a ventilation fan, with four sails on the end of the fan shaft where it protrudes from the box. The box is mounted on what superficially appears to be a post, giving rise to the assumption that this was a post mill, but which Hills suggests is actually a trunk to take the air into the mine. This structure is still at least one step away from a hollow post mill.

The option of the mill at Wollaton being a tower mill cannot be summarily dismissed. Stone is known to have been used later for mill building in Nottinghamshire and the small cylindrical tower mill was known in England at that date. What is possibly the oldest surviving example, thought to date from 1367, stands at Burton Dassett in the Midlands. And, as we have seen, it was the tower mill which the Scottish owners later used at their mines. There are thus some interesting options as to what this wind engine looked like, but in the absence of further evidence we cannot reach a conclusion. This wind engine is almost certainly an example of an industrialist being at the forefront of windmill technology.

The non-ferrous metal mines also met problems with invasive water and Cornish tin mines have made use of wind-powered pumps on occasions. A writer in *The Mining Journal*, 1879, said that, 'We are glad to see an indication, or rather promise, of fresh economies in the revival of the proposals to use wind power in mines, Cornwall is quite as windy as Wales, all things considered ...'

Three specific examples are given by Douch (*Cornish Windmills*). Firstly, some time before 1711, a wind-powered pump was in use at a tin mine at Tremenheere. At this date the installation of the first Newcomen engine in a Cornish mine was still some five years away.

Secondly, it is known that in 1752 a Dr William Borlase '... saw a wind engine, like a windmill with fanes, 2 miles before St Austle – but when the water was drawn out they could not check it. Whilst it worked it drew out more than the fire engines, but now idle – It wants a counterpoise when there is no water.'

The third was erected in 1797 at the Ding Dong Mine to the north of Penzance, as the following interesting account recalls: 'Captain Trevithick at that time put a wind engine in the mine, sometimes it went so fast that they could not stop it; some sailors came from Penzance and made a plan for reefing the sails.'

The question of the windmill running away when the load was taken off it was obviously a serious problem for the miners and, in 1787, Benjamin Heame, a local merchant, patented a system to overcome the problem. His plan was to use sails '... made to hoist and lower, as lug sails, try sails, or of various other forms ...' connected by the striking rod arrangement of Lee to balance-weights hanging at the rear (Patent No 1588, 1 February 1787). This arrangement is not known outside Cornwall and in any event would have been overtaken by Hooper's patent which, of course, raises the interesting question of whether this problem was brought to Captain Hooper's attention by the 'sailors' of Penzance?

Finally, there may have been one example in Cornwall of wind power being used to crush ore. T.R. Harris has drawn attention to a patent taken out by John Rowe in 1757 (Patent No 715, 27 May 1757) for a method of grinding mineral ore. It is stated to be

> ... as any common mill for corn or grist, either with wind or water ... with such sort of stones and hung in the same manner and principle, but the inside of such stones, between them, are fixed or inlaid with iron, faced with steel half ways ... and the mill's mouth where the ore is delivered, hangs a copper or iron sieve for sifting and sizing the ore ...

Rowe claims to have erected such a mill but rather frustratingly does not say whether it was powered by wind or water.

Another mining area where wind power was tried were the lead mines of Flintshire. The first was at Trelogan mine, owned by the London (Quaker) Lead Company. In 1730 they erected a wind-powered pump but this proved to be inadequate, being replaced by a Newcomen-type steam engine in 1732. The windmill may have continued to work in conjunction with the steam engine, as both were still in existence in 1735. The windmill was a small tower mill with four common sails and winded by tailpole. Secondly, at Cadole near Loggerheads, Edward Cheney operated a lead mine during the 1730s which had a windmill operating a pump, thought to be a rag and chain pump. Unfortunately, Cheney was soon in financial difficulties and in 1741 the wind engine was listed among goods seized in lieu of debts. The third wind-powered pump was used during the 18th century at Bryn Goch mine near Garreg where several mines were being worked. The mill was still in existence in 1874. It is also reported that a windmill was used at a mine in Flintshire for dressing ore.

Mining in Wales also means gold. During the 19th century a wind-powered pump was used at the Clogau Gold Mine which still existed at the site in 1901, although by that date in ruins.

In the mid-18th century, Charles Roe was involved in developing the major copper mine at Parys Mountain on Anglesey (see page 84). The ore was found very close to the surface and was first worked by open cast methods. As the excavation grew deeper, miners were lowered into the pits by small hand-operated winches, a dramatic but slow and dangerous method of working. Water was a problem, always threatening to flood the pits and by 1785 a wind-powered pump had been erected at the site to keep the workings free of water. The mill was still in use in 1788 but disappeared shortly afterwards as the area of the open cast expanded.

But that was not the end of wind power at Parys Mountain. A steam engine had been installed at Cairn's shaft (vestiges of the engine house can still be made out) which proved successful in controlling the water (as well as raising men and ore). But it was expensive to run, coal having to be brought overland by horse and cart. By the 1870s, the economics of the mine were becoming difficult, and consequently in 1878 the company built a windmill at the high point on the mountain (or what was left of it) which they connected to the pumps by some 200 feet of timber flat rods. The windmill proved to be highly successful, saving considerably on costs, and remained in use until about 1905.

It is not known who built this mill but it is of particular interest as it does not follow the established design of windmills on Anglesey. It was built of rubblestone, some 30 feet to the curb, with a pent roofed cap, common sails and winded by chain wheel, so far standard Anglesey practice. But the different feature was that it had five sails. The mill was clearly built by a local millwright but one who was aware of Smeaton's ideas, and who was capable of producing a successful windmill.

We have seen that the Firth of Forth in Scotland was an area where wind power seems to have been attractive and it is known that the Earl of Hopetoun used wind power for grinding and refining lead ore at Leith, near Edinburgh, during the 18th century.

Many mines used water power for pumping and processing ores, in some cases constructing extremely long leats to tap distant water sources; with careful management and co-operation, it was possible to squeeze the last drop of energy out of a very limited source. The same criteria applied to quarries, particularly the slate quarries of north and central Wales. For example, in the Nantlle Valley, a small lake formed by the run-off from surrounding hills was led through five separate quarries, where it drove in succession some ten water wheels before discharging into the stream on the valley floor. Water management of this type calls for able surveying and engineering. But it also calls for an amicable working arrangement between the quarry owners who make use of the water supply. In one case this relationship broke down and as a result the water supply to Hafod Las Quarry, where it was used for pumping, was cut off. To remedy the situation a wind engine was built in 1802, which comprised a small stone tower, with four sails and a simple pent-roof cap, winded by tail pole. Unfortunately, as the depth of the quarry increased, the power requirements also increased and the wind engine was replaced by steam in 1812.

We can assume that, during the ten years of its working life, the wind engine at Hafod Las was successful, as in 1806 an adjoining quarry, Cilgwyn, high up on the valley side, decided to follow suit. The engine was built by John Hughes, a local blacksmith, and we have a good description of the structure. It comprised a base stone wall, about five feet high, on top of which four strong timbers supported the framework for the windshaft. The pump rod descended vertically through the rock

48 Drawing of pumping mill at Hafod Las Slate Quarry, built c.1802. Detail from a drawing by Cornelius Varley, c.1802.

below the engine, possibly driven by a cranked windshaft, similar to the cranks used at the pumps driven by water wheels. We also know the mill had common sails, probably four, and was probably winded by tailpole. The cost of the engine was £120 and Hughes was also obliged to pay half the cost of maintaining and carrying out any repairs (except for sail cloth) for a period of five years.

A third quarry in Nantlle vale used wind power, namely Braich Rhydd, where a wind pump was erected in 1827, but this only seems to have been used for a short period.

At the Rosebush Slate Quarry in Pembrokeshire, a windmill was built to drive dressing machines. Unfortunately, the structure was damaged in a gale before the drive shaft could be devised, and consequently it was never put into use.

One other quarry had a similar problem, the South Barrule Slate Quarry on the Isle of Man. Here an extremely small windmill was built in 1902, a tower mill of local stone (slate) some 20 to 25 feet to the curb standing on a rectangular base 13 feet square. The north and south faces of the base each have a pair of vertical slots, 4ft 4ins high by 12 inches wide (one on the north side now blocked up). The western wall contains an opening some 18 inches by 12 inches which is in line with the probable location of the upright shaft. There is a doorway centrally located on the eastern side and a blocked up doorway on the western side. It seems likely that a horizontal pulley was mounted at the lower end of the upright shaft, from which a drive would be taken by an endless rope through one or both of the two pairs of vertical slots. The opening in the western wall may have taken a layshaft to take power off the spur wheel, using bevel gears, for use outside the tower.

The tower is located to the south of the quarry and, rather unusually, well below the skyline. Between the tower and the quarry a shallow trench suggests that a drive, probably a wire rope rather than flatrods, ran to the quarry.

The use of the windmill is far from certain. One suggestion is to power an incline drawing slate wagons out of the pit workings. This must be a possibility, as the evidence indicates a continuous rope drive passing round a horizontal pulley (sheave) fixed to the lower end of the upright shaft, through the slots in the north wall, then along the trench and into the quarry. It is also claimed that the mill drove two saw tables used to cut slate blocks to size, which could account for the small opening in the western face, through which a layshaft would take the drive to the saw tables. Having said that, there is no evidence of sawn off-cuts which one normally finds around the site of a slate mill. Neither of these two explanations accounts for the slots in the south wall.

49 Tower of windmill at South Barrule Slate Quarry, Isle of Man, built *c*.1902.

As with most slate quarries, it would be necessary to pump water out of the workings, for which wind power would be most suitable. Such pump could have been driven by the endless rope, but a more usual arrangement would have been a crank at the foot of the upright shaft to produce a reciprocating motion. (If the use was changed from winding to pumping, using some form of crank, this might explain why only one of the slots in the northern face was blocked up.)

Consequently, we remain uncertain as to the purpose of this mill. Having regard to the size and location of the structure, there must be considerable uncertainty as to whether it ever provided sufficient power to perform. The empty tower remains in situ.

Not far away, at Billown Quarry, a large iron wind pump was used for drainage. Whilst not strictly a moveable structure, it was de-mountable, and was moved around the quarry as the need arose.

Finally, the Scottish Industrial Archaeological Survey have identified three stone quarries where wind power was used to de-water the excavations (the towers of which still survived in the 1980s). The first was at Dunbar, again on the Firth of Forth. The tower stood some 14 feet high with an external diameter of 9ft 6ins at the base, and was built of rubble stone but with dressed red sandstone at the top to hold the curb. There were no windows but a single door at ground-floor level. There are nine holes around the tower some 20 inches above ground level, which may have held a stage. Why a stage would be needed at such a low level is uncertain but the mill is built on a slope, which might have made it difficult to access the sails on the down-hill side without a platform.

50 Drawing of pumping mill as used at mines around the Firth of Forth during the 18th century.

The other two mills were at flagstone quarries around Thurso on the northern coast of Caithness. One, at the Hill of Forss Quarries, was 19 feet high and 12ft 6ins external diameter at the base. The other, known as Castlehill Windmill, was 17 feet high and 11ft 10ins in diameter at the base. Both are sturdily built, of local flagstone, with the walls around six feet thick at the base. These two mills were, of course, sited in extremely exposed positions and were obviously built to withstand strong winds. Unfortunately, we have no information as to the type of sails used but they would have been comparatively small, no more than twenty feet in length.

8

Paper Making

Paper is one of those commodities which are so common as to be absolutely taken for granted but without which, even in the day of the computer and all that goes with it, government, commerce, not to mention education, would come to a halt. Its wide application results in paper being produced in a variety of qualities, including brown paper, still used in many stores for wrapping goods, white paper for printing and writing letters, and special paper for such items as banknotes and toilet paper.

Paper making was late to arrive in England, the first paper mill being established in 1494, by which date paper mills were already well established in France, Germany, Italy and Spain. Indeed, when Caxton opened his first printing press in 1476, he had to rely on imported paper.

At that date, paper was made from cellulose fibres, which were derived from a number of second-hand sources, e.g. disused sails from ships, old hemp ropes and, most commonly of all, from old clothes. The first stage in the process was to wash and sort the rags. No bleaches were available so consequently white paper could only be made from white rags. Up to the 16th century, rags were cut up into small pieces and then macerated, using hammer-type stampers. This part of the operation required considerable power and the hammers were driven in the manner common in iron forges, being lifted by cams on a shaft, which then fell under their own weight. Whilst being beaten the rags were placed in a stone tub, filled with water, the resultant pulp then being transferred to a storage vat. Individual sheets of paper were formed by dipping a shallow tray, the base of which comprised a wire sieve, into the pulp and, after lifting out of the pulp, allowing surplus water to drain away. The resultant layer of pulp was the sheet of paper but still in a rather mushy state. The 'sheet' was placed on a piece of felt and a 'sandwich' was built up, of felt, sheet, felt, sheet etc., in the trade called a post. When a sufficiently large post had been assembled, it was placed in a hand press to squeeze out the remainder of the water, then hung up in a drying loft until completely dry. The drying lofts were usually at first-floor level, the walls of which were fitted with vertical adjustable louvres, which gave these mills a distinctive appearance. Wherever possible the stampers were driven by a water wheel.

The first English paper mill was established at Hertford in 1494 by John Tate, who took over and converted a water-powered corn mill on the Beane, a tributary of the River Lea, and he would have used the process described above. Other mills appeared, the majority in the London area, possibly making use of disused mill sites such as the former iron forges in Kent. Most of these early mills seem to have been short-lived. Alfred Shorter (*Water Paper Mills In England*) states that it was not until 1588 that a permanent paper mill was established, at Dartford in Kent. During the first half of the 17th century there were around forty paper mills in England, which R. Hills (*Paper making in Britain 1588-1988*) suggests had risen to 116 by 1700 and 4,127 by 1800. However, there are difficulties with these figures as it is not clear how long these mills survived; thus the number in operation at any one time was probably fewer than the quoted figures.

Mills using the stamper press would have had a very limited output. It is claimed that it would take up to 36 hours to fully macerate one tub of rags. By the mid-17th century, a major improvement to the process had appeared in Holland, generally referred to as the Hollander tub or Hollander beater, which replaced the stampers. This machine comprised a wooden tub, rectangular in plan but with the two short ends semi-circular, and with a dividing wall down part of the centre. Across one side of the tub bronze bars were fixed into the base, above which a drum rotated, with similar bars set into its circumference. The rags were placed in the tub, water was added, and the drum made to rotate. Thus the rags were ripped by the action of the bars on the drum and the base, the movement of the drum also causing the pulp to circulate round the tub. This system, introduced into England around 1730, was claimed to produce eight times the quantity of pulp produced using stampers, and continued in use well into the 19th century. Examples of this system can be seen in operation at Wookey Hole in Somerset and the *Openluchtmuseum* at Arnhem in Holland.

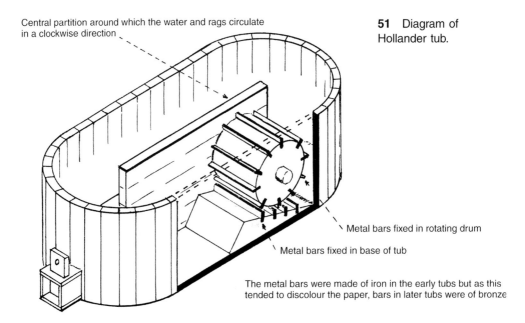

Central partition around which the water and rags circulate in a clockwise direction

51 Diagram of Hollander tub.

Metal bars fixed in rotating drum

Metal bars fixed in base of tub

The metal bars were made of iron in the early tubs but as this tended to discolour the paper, bars in later tubs were of bronze

During the 18th century the major market for paper was London. By virtue of its large population it was also a prime source of raw materials – rags. It is not surprising, therefore, that a high percentage of the early paper mills were established within travelling distance of the capital. But the capital also had a large demand for most other products, so consequently there was a considerable pressure on water power sites in and around the area. In an attempt to overcome this problem wind power was tried. The earliest reference to a wind-powered paper mill occurs in 1710. Farries and Mason (*Windmills of Surrey and Inner London*) state that

> Sutton Nicholls, in his *View of London from the Temple to the Tower* published in 1710, shows a tower mill with four cloth sails standing in Blackfriars Road just to the west of Christ Church. It is described as 'Paper Mill' and appears again in a panorama by the same artist in 1724, but there all knowledge of it ends.

Richard Hills (*Power from the Wind*) mentions two further wind mills in the south-east – the first stood at Deptford near the East India Docks. It was insured with the Sun Fire Alliance Company in 1751, which was rather fortuitous as the premises were destroyed by fire four years later. It must have been rebuilt as it is mentioned, for the last time, in an insurance policy dated November 1777. It can be assumed that this mill was in operation for over 26 years and was probably subsumed into later redevelopment schemes for the area.

The second wind-powered paper mill mentioned by Hills was at Cheriton in Kent. This mill is given a brief mention by several authors but the only detailed account of it occurs in Hasted's *History of Kent*, published in 1799, which states that the mill was essentially a watermill on the Seabrook, a short stream which tumbles from the North Downs into the sea at Folkestone and that at that time a rather unusual device was employed so that the mill could obtain motive power from either water or wind. The exact nature of the 'unusual device' is not recorded. The chalky water would be good for paper making but the supply would probably have been insufficient to meet the demands of both the process and the water wheel at all times, hence the windmill.

North of the capital, in Northampton, a watermill built in the 16th century to grind corn had by 1780 been converted to a paper mill, in which year it was badly damaged by fire. In 1702, a spring had been discovered nearby which provided drinking water to a fountain in the town square. To pump the water a windmill was built in 1719, a three-storey squat structure built of local stone and fitted with four common sails. The water supply scheme was abandoned in 1745 but, when the paper mill was subsequently rebuilt, the windmill was connected to it in some way, as an advertisement in the local press claimed that the paper mill was capable of being powered by wind, water or both. The new mill only operated for fewer than twenty years as by 1788 it had reverted to corn milling, still using both power sources.

Two interesting references to wind-powered paper mills occur in Birmingham. The first, known as Easy Hill, was a small tower mill, built around 1748, for John

Baskerville, a famous printer of his day. Baskerville was very much a free thinker, with a lifestyle which incurred censure from his contemporaries. One result of this is that, as it was not until the 20th century that biographers produced an account and assessment of his work, the passage of time has obscured details of the history of the mill. In his will (made in 1773) Baskerville refers to 'a conical building on my own premises, heretofore used as a mill' without being more specific. In 1836 a writer refers to it as a 'paper mill'. A contemporary claimed that Baskerville manufactured his own paper and Baskerville himself talked about paper 'of his own manufacture'. But F.E. Pardoe (*John Baskerville of Birmingham: Letter-Founder and Printer*) asserts that it is likely

> he could not have made more than a few sheets at Easy Hill. One of the essentials in paper making is a copious supply of water, and although there were two pumps and a fish pond at Easy Hill, a rather greater supply was normally needed for paper making on a commercial scale.

Pardoe also points out that Baskerville often referred to the cost of paper in terms which suggest he was buying it from suppliers. Nevertheless, correspondence clearly indicates that Baskerville was supplying quality writing paper to various retailers, which may have been produced at the mill in small quantities.

One of Baskerville's innovations was the design of a typeface with very narrow lines, but which he found difficult to print on the paper then available. To solve the problem he enlisted the help of the leading paper maker James Whatman (of Turkey Paper Mill in Kent), who produced the smoother 'wove' paper. ('Wove' refers to the base of the tray in which the sheet of paper is produced – it does not indicate the paper was in some way woven.)

However the mill was used during his lifetime, it was put to a unique use on his death, which can best be described by the following extract from his will:

52 Sketch of Baskerville's Paper Mill by Joseph McKenna, after conversion to a mausoleum. The mill was built *c.*1748.

'... that my Executors do cause my body to be buried in a conical building in my premises, heretofore used as a mill, which I have lately raised higher and painted, and in a vault which I have prepared for it.' This conical building is shown in a drawing by David Oates dated 1789 from which it appears that the mill was originally a fairly squat tower mill, about 18 to 20 feet to the curb. When Baskerville converted it to a mausoleum, he added a conical roof surmounted by a lantern, which more than doubled the height of the structure.

The second mill in Birmingham stood in Birchfield Road, built in 1759, a tower mill somewhat resembling the ubiquitous bottle kiln found in the potteries. It was built for the Birmingham historian, William Hutton, who wanted to produce paper cheaply. Joseph McKenna (*Windmills in the Black Country*) states that Hutton was convinced that his employees were cheating him and within two years the project was abandoned. The mill was sold in 1763 and converted to a dwelling, in which use it remained until the end of the 19th century.

The last wind-powered paper mill to be built, and perhaps the most important in the present context, stood on Beverley Road in Hull. By the late 18th century, as we have seen in chapter 2 on oil seed crushing, the town, which had no water power sites, was the scene of some very efficient state-of-the-art windmills, most probably built by the Hull millwrights, Norman and Smithson.

The nearest paper mills to the town were at Driffield, some 20 miles to the north, and at Barrow across the Humber estuary, both water powered and the latter owned by Messrs Howard and Houghton. It is probable that this mill had a very limited water supply, as in 1786 the firm decided to build a steam-powered paper mill in Hull. For this purpose they purchased a steam engine from Boulton & Watt (rated at 10hp), the first use of steam power in the paper making industry. The plans of the engine and mill are preserved in the Boulton & Watt archive at Birmingham Central Library, from which we have a clear picture of the machinery installed. The engine drove two Hollander tubs, each being at the head of a production line. From each tub, the pulp flowed into a 'stuff chest' where it was stored pending transfer to the vats, two rectangular vats on one of the production lines, an almost circular vat on the other. At the end of each line stood a hand operated press. (In fact, it appears from an advertisement dated 1799 that by that date the mill was fitted with four vats.)

This was clearly a serious attempt at stepping up output. Hills states that possibly three-quarters of the paper mills built up to 1800 had only one vat and that, in 1805, the 461 paper mills which had received licences had an average of 1.5 vats. The millwright for this scheme was J. Moyser, who had built the paper mill at Driffield, and it is interesting to note from correspondence between Moyser and Boulton & Watt that consideration had been given to using wind power to support the steam engine, but this was not pursued. Howard and Houghton probably regretted this decision, as by 1799 the concern was bankrupt and the steam engine was subsequently sold in 1802 to J. & H. Lodge of Halifax.

During this period the firm of Norman and Smithson had become established millwrights in Hull, and had built a number of mills, for both corn milling and

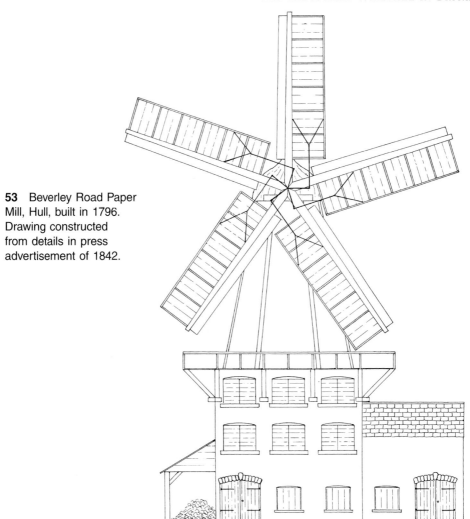

53 Beverley Road Paper Mill, Hull, built in 1796. Drawing constructed from details in press advertisement of 1842.

other industrial uses. In 1796 they built the wind-powered paper mill on Beverley Road, Stepney, the area into which Hull was expanding. The mill was a tower mill described as being eight storeys high, the first, second and third floors being 30ft square. This seems to follow the example of Smeaton and it is probable that the upper floors were built of timber – in effect, a smock mill. This would be a sensible arrangement as the upper floors in the tower, which in a corn mill would be used to store grain, would have no corresponding use in a paper mill. It is possible that these upper floors could have been used for drying paper but it might be inconvenient to carry sheets of wet paper up narrow stepladders. Assuming the Hollander tub and the vats were on the ground floor, it is possible that the two upper floors of the rectangular base were used as drying lofts.

The mill had five roller sails, each roller being six feet wide with movable weather boards on each leading edge. The windshaft was of cast iron. The sails were removed in 1848 but the premises continued as a paper mill until the second half of the 20th century.

The mill was located adjacent to the Cottingham Drain (which carried surface water). The paper-making process required copious amounts of water (something like 30,000 gallons to produce one ton of paper). The water used for washing would need to be disposed of. The public water supply would not have reached the mill by this date, so water may have been drawn either from a well on site or possibly from the drain. The waste water must certainly have been discharged into the drain.

Unfortunately, there is no indication of the internal layout of the mill but it would certainly have had at least one Hollander tub. The Howard and Houghton mill had two, driven by a 10hp steam engine, and there is no reason to assume that a windmill of the size mentioned above was not capable of producing equivalent power; consequently it is quite probable that the wind-powered paper mill also had two tubs and four vats.

The very interesting question is, what motivated Norman and Smithson to build this mill? There are at least two possibilities. First, as has been mentioned, by the mid-1790s the firm had established a thriving practice as millwrights, building some substantial windmills. But also in the mid-1780s three of the new Boulton & Watt engines had been installed in the town – did they see this as a threat to their business – did they set out to show what wind power could do? If so, it might be argued that this showed the firm in a less than progressive light, which would be contrary to the evidence. The second possibility is perhaps more likely. Surprisingly, Robert Smithson came from a family of paper makers in Skipton and by the start of the 19th century the firm was starting to diversify. James Norman had several commissions in the wider field of civil engineering, i.e. he rebuilt North Bridge and built the new Ferry Boat Dock (both of which involved using heavy timbers, a field in which the firm had considerable expertise). Did Smithson therefore decide to go back into his original business? He certainly seems to have been active in the paper-making business and some years later his son followed him into it. It must, however, be noted that the millwrighting partnership continued until the death of the partners; as late as 1819 they built the Maud Foster Mill and in 1821 Skidby Mill, both of which survive to this day.

Whatever the reason for building the paper mill, it was certainly a successful venture. The steam-powered mill went out of business shortly afterwards but the wind-powered mill continued under wind power for almost fifty years!

Finally, an article in the Newcastle press of December 1866 records the demise of a windmill used in connection with the manufacture of paper. The mill was built originally as a corn mill near the area known as Byker Hill and comprised a tall brick tower mill of six storeys, fitted with four sails. At some date a gentleman by the name of John Brown had established what was described as a 'manufactory of substances', ground from chaff, sawdust and the like, which substances were used for the making of coarse paper. At some stage a steam engine had been added but the whole operation was destroyed by fire in December 1866.

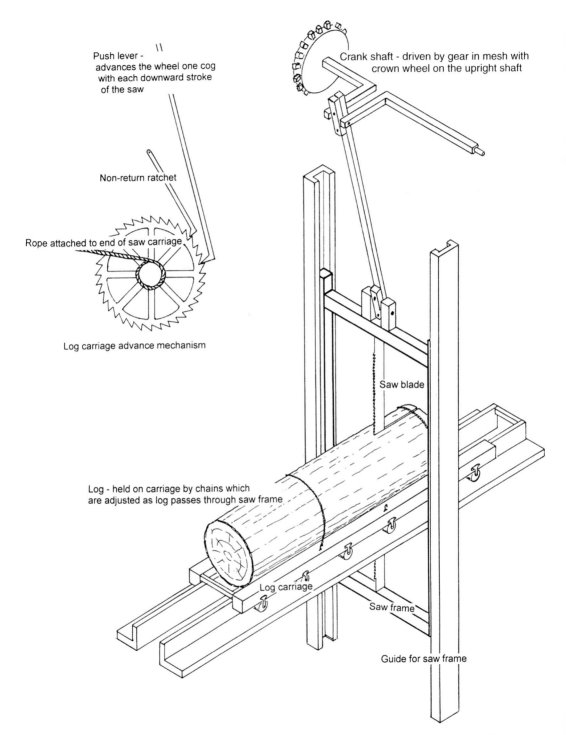

Push lever -
advances the wheel one cog
with each downward stroke
of the saw

Crank shaft - driven by gear in mesh with
crown wheel on the upright shaft

Non-return ratchet

Rope attached to end of saw carriage

Log carriage advance mechanism

Saw blade

Log - held on carriage by chains which
are adjusted as log passes through saw frame

Log carriage

Saw frame

Guide for saw frame

54 Diagram of saw frame. The drawing shows only one saw blade but in most cases there
would be several, in some cases sufficient to reduce a log to floor-board size planks at one
pass through the saws.

9

Timber Trades

In England, from early times, forests have been cleared to make way for settlements and agriculture; timber has been felled to build houses and ships, and it has been used as a fuel for both domestic and industrial use. By the start of the 18th century, leaving aside the special woods used by cabinet makers, England was having to import a large amount of basic timber from the Baltic countries and North America. During this period all work with timber was done manually, including the basic reduction of logs using the ubiquitous pit saw.

Holland was in a similar position but for a different reason. Until the 14th century most of North Holland was little more than marsh land. Thereafter the policy of draining polders, using exclusively wind power, produced considerable areas of *terra firma*. Timber was used extensively, again for building homes and ships, imported from various parts of the world, much of it through the Zaan district and it is here that the wind-powered sawmills first appeared. The idea was patented in 1592 (in Holland) and thereafter two types of sawmill appeared, the well-known paltrok mill in about 1600, and the later smock mill version. Dealing first with the general mechanism, which is common to both, the sawmill was essentially a mechanised pit saw. A number of saw blades were fixed into a rectangular timber frame, which was mounted in vertical guide slots. The upright shaft carried a trundle gear wheel a few feet below the wallower, which meshed with a lantern pinion on a horizontal cranked shaft, the number of cranks being dependent upon the number of saw frames. In one of the famous Dutch mill books, van Zyl illustrates a sawmill with three frames carrying in total 21 saw blades, the blades being spaced differently in each frame, to enable planks to be cut to different thicknesses. Thus, as the sails turned, the frames moved up and down to make the cutting stroke. The log to be sawn was mounted on a carriage or carriages, running on rails, which fed the log into the saws. The carriage was inched forward by a ratchet device on each cutting stroke.

In Holland, logs were often floated to the sawmills as rafts and had to remain in the water for some time before they were sawn. For this reason sawmills were always located along a water front, sometimes almost totally surrounded by water.

Although the internal machinery is identical in both mill types, the basic structure has important differences. The paltrok mill has a body which is rectangular in plan, with what may best be described as a shed extending at each side. This gives cover to the carriage platform. The tower has no separate cap and the framework which holds the windshaft is part of the main structure of the tower. But, as it is still essential that the sails be kept facing into wind, the whole structure is mounted on a circular brick base, which has a series of rollers on its top surface, on which the mill rests. Thus, to wind the mill, the entire unit is turned, on the rollers, with the aid of a winch. To lift logs out of the water, the mill has a crane at the end of the platform from which the logs are presented to the saw frame, also driven by the sails. Excellent examples of the paltrok mill can be seen in Holland, at the Arnhem Open Air Museum and Zaans Schans.

The paltrok mill usually has only two or three frames. Where a greater capacity was required, the second type, the smock sawmill, was built. The internal layout is identical, but this type of sawmill has a normal smock, with a cap, and the whole structure stands on the ground (or, more precisely, as the mills are built at the water's edge and therefore susceptible to flooding, they are usually raised on brick pillars). To raise the logs out of the water, a slipway is provided, with a powered winch.

This Dutch sawmill proved to be very successful and the concept spread to other parts of Europe, particularly the forest regions of the Russian North and the Baltic States, usually based on the smock mill arrangement, not the paltrok. In some cases these mills are quite small, mostly having only one saw frame.

55 Seventeenth-century saw mill at Lambeth. This is probably a Dutch-style paltrok mill. Detail from an engraving by Schenk.

The idea came to England in 1658, when a wind-powered sawmill was built at Lambeth. A contemporary engraving by Peter Schenk shows this mill, which is certainly Dutch in design, though it is not clear which of the two types it is. It has the appearance of a smock mill but has no tailpole, so the possibility that it was a paltrok mill cannot be dismissed. Farries and Mason recount that Oliver Cromwell is reputed to have visited this mill and was so pleased with it that he had it 'confirmed by Parliament', which perhaps indicates who the sawyers supported in the Civil War? (However, no record of the statute has been found.) There may have been two further sawmills at Lambeth. Throughout the 18th century there were several timber yards along the Thames (between what would later be the sites of Waterloo and Westminster Bridges) and Farries and

Mason claim that two of these had sawmills, although they do not give any authority for this claim. It appears that these mills were hollow post mills, the saw frames being located in the roundhouse. All three sawmills in Lambeth had disappeared by *c.*1750.

When the first of these mills was built, there was considerable opposition from the sawyers, who (rightly) predicted that the new device would put them out of work. Fortunately, the protection of Cromwell seems to have prevented any action but in the neighbouring area of Limehouse the sawyers were more militant. A wind-powered sawmill built in 1663 immediately ran into trouble, being attacked by the sawyers and abandoned. A century later, in 1767, a second wind-powered sawmill was built on the same site. This project was financed by a merchant by the name of Charles Dingley and built by James Stansfield, a carpenter from Bingley in Yorkshire, who had apparently made a study of sawmills in Holland and Norway. It contained 36 saws (probably on three frames) and was claimed to be 'much more useful' than the Dutch sawmills on which it was modelled. The building cost £4,454 but it too suffered damage at the hands of the mob in 1768 and a further £1,123 was expended on repairs, the mill being out of action for six months. In spite of this extremely high cost, it only had a brief working life, as in 1795 it was observed that it '... still exists, but has not been employed for many years'.

The next wind-powered sawmill in England was built in Hull in *c.*1796 for William Osborne, a major timber merchant and town councillor, the millwrights almost certainly being Norman and Smithson. In 1819 an advertisement in the local press stated that the mill had eight sails and, assuming it had eight sails when built, they must surely have been roller sails. Unfortunately, the mill was severely damaged in a gale in the 1820s and went out of use.

Hull exemplifies a further point about the application of power in the timber trade. It was one of the major centres for the importation of timber from the Baltic (in 1823 there were some 32 timber merchants in the town) but in 1820 an engineer named Richard Witty, who 20 years earlier had set up in business in Hull as a maker of steam engines, left Hull to try his luck in the Potteries, a move ascribed by a local economic historian to the fact that the application of steam power in the town was slow, particularly in the corn milling and timber sawing industries. Why it should be slow is a matter of conjecture. It could be continued opposition from the sawyers (Osborne's mill was built for the specific task of cutting veneers so the sawyers might not have seen this as quite such a threat); it could be reluctance on the part of the merchants to invest capital; or, of course, it could be related to the efficiency of the windmills being built in Hull at this date!

It is interesting to speculate on where Osborne picked up the idea of building a wind-powered sawmill; he would almost certainly have known of the adventures in London and he might well have seen the sawmills in Holland, from contact with Dutch timber merchants. But it is quite possible that his Hull mill had closer links with Scotland. We have seen that wind power was being used there to a limited degree. Around 1786 a company owned by Osborne and a partner from York had purchased an extensive forest at Glenmoor in Strathspey on the Murray Firth, for its timber. To house their workmen they built the town of Kingston and to convert the timber they built two sawmills, one powered by water, the other by wind. The latter had between 36 and 40 saws and must have been similar in design to the non-paltrock type of Dutch sawmill.

In Hull, Osborne had a fairly close working relationship with James Norman, who no doubt bought timber from him, but Norman was only at the beginning of his career in 1786 and it must be unlikely that he was involved. Anderson (*A History of Scottish Forestry*) states that the use of wind power for timber sawing was known in Scotland, for example at Airth, built by 1723. The best known example stood at Broughty Castle, built originally for wood turning but at the end of its life used for making matchboxes. This was only a small cylindrical tower but fitted with five sails, probably spring sails. (It will be remembered that the spring sail was invented by the Scottish engineer, Andrew Meikle.) The conclusion must nevertheless be that the sawmill at Strathspey was built by a Scottish millwright.

We know Osborne's sawmill in Hull was built to cut veneers but we do not know what machinery was used for this purpose. Vertical saws would probably do the job perfectly well but some 20 years earlier a new device had been patented by Samuel Miller: the circular saw (Patent No 1152, 11 April 1777). Miller's patent proposed that the saw should be powered by a horizontal windmill but there is no evidence that such a structure was ever built. In fact it was Walter Taylor, a Southampton carpenter, who, in 1781, first used a circular saw, at a converted watermill on the River Itchen, where he used the saw for making ships' blocks (for the rigging). This proved highly efficient, and was subsequently followed by Samuel Bentham and Marc Brunel (father of the GWR engineer). But, apart from this application, the circular saw did not come into common use until the 19th century. Nor did the circular saw entirely supersede the saw frame; the latter was still a better tool for reducing large logs, but it did make a mechanised saw available to the whole range of trades involved in working with wood, down to the smallest joiner's shop. Provided, of course, they had power available.

In some parts of the country, wind power was still an attractive option and, at the start of the 19th century, it was to become even more so. The issue of self-regulating sails was still concerning the minds of millers and millwrights. Hooper had produced a practical arrangement but the cloths deteriorated quickly on exposure to the elements and required constant attention. The answer eventually came in 1807 when William Cubitt, a Suffolk millwright, combined Hooper's striking mechanism with the shuttered sail put forward by Meikle fifty years earlier, and produced the self-regulating shuttered sail which became almost universal in England and Wales, and is generally known simply as the patent sail (Patent No 3041, 9 May 1807). The patent sail was the final stage in the evolution of the English windmill.

Timber has always been an important building material. During the 18th and 19th centuries, in the south-east of England it was used not only for the basic frame but also as cladding, in the form of overlapping horizontal planks known as clap boarding. The windmill itself gives a first-hand example of this; it is significant that the smock mill, which is essentially a clap-boarded tower mill, proliferated in south-east England, from the Wash to Southampton. Many of the watermills in this area were of similar construction, along with countless barns and other farm buildings.

Norwich was a town which, at the start of the 19th century, had a population of 36,000 and was still one of the largest towns in Britain. It soon fell behind as towns in the North and Midlands developed but during the 19th century many new houses were built. Whereas brick was coming into general use, there was still a demand for timber. So far as power was concerned, the town had its water-powered corn mill on the River Wessum and there were further water mills on the River Yare to the south (one of which at some stage was used as a sawmill). In 1802 a steam-powered subscription mill was erected near Black Friars Bridge. But on the higher ground across the Wessum, to the north and east, at least two post mills had existed for some time, also producing flour, one being the well known Sprowston Mill.

By the mid-19th century, there were a number of timber merchants in Norwich, who operated wind-powered sawmills on this higher ground. One such, Bailey Bird, had two in Philadelphia Lane in 1845, one with three saws, the other with two. Following his death in 1860, the mills were purchased by Samuel Cann, who, having sold one of the mills in 1876, was still in business at the other in the 1880s. In addition, two wind corn mills, which stood on Gas Hill, were converted to saw milling. The first was a smock mill, possibly built in the 1790s. Conversion took place in 1847 but does not appear to have been successful as, when it was advertised for sale in 1850, it was to be removed from the site. The second mill on Gas Hill was built in 1830 as a corn mill and converted to saw milling sometime between 1837 and 1856. By 1859 it was occupied by George Gallant and remained in his family until sold on the death of his son in 1899. In the press advertisement the site was described as a 'timber merchants premises' which indicates a reasonably sized concern.

These four mills were either built or converted for sole use as sawmills, but there are many examples across the country of a circular saw being mounted on a small frame and added to an existing mill (both wind and water), and both uses continued in tandem. The sawmill may have been for the miller's own use or for the general benefit of local people. An example occurred at Hellesden, just outside Norwich, where a four-storey smock mill on Drayton High Road had a saw fitted. The mill was dismantled in 1838 and may have been re-erected in Drayton Village.

Also near Norwich, at Sprowston, two tower mills were built by 1826 of similar design, fitted with circular saws, although one had disappeared by 1864. Of similar date a sawmill had been built at Pulham Market, in this case a four-storey eight-sided smock mill. Steam power was added in 1883 but the windmill continued in use for several years. At Cawston a four-storey brick tower mill was built in

56 Cawston Saw Mill, Norfolk, built 1853. Note the identical external appearance of the saw mill on the right and the corn mill on the left.

the 1820s, again with a Norfolk cap, four double-sided patent sails and fantail, which used circular saws to make herring boxes, being owned at that date by the Bailey Bird who also owned the sawmills in Norwich, mentioned above. This mill was later converted to corn milling which continued well into the 20th century.

Berney Arms Mill at Reedham had been built c.1797 for use in connection with the manufacture of cement. But by 1828 it had in addition been fitted out with '... seven circular saws and a deal frame particularly adapted for sawing for Herring Barrels, in which a very considerable trade is now carried on'. It is assumed that the reference to a deal frame implies a log carriage and not a vertical saw frame. The mill was demolished in the 1860s, to be replaced by the present mill on the site (see page 59).

In neighbouring Suffolk, a six-sided smock mill at Southtown, built by 1825, was occupied by Fellowes, Barth and Palmer, timber merchants, which may indicate its use as a sawmill. A large ten-sided smock mill (only one of three which were not octagonal) was built at Wangford in 1843, on the Earl of Stradbroke's estate. The cant posts were some 40 feet long and the span of the sails approximately 80 feet. At ground level a wide opening gave access to the log carriage, which may indicate that the mill was fitted with a saw frame for the basic reduction of logs felled on the estate (as was the case of the water-powered sawmill at Gunton Park built c.1820). In the 1860s three pairs of stones were added to grind corn and the mill continued in dual use until destroyed by fire in 1928. It is understood that there was also a smock built sawmill at Wisbech.

Kent is a county where wind power was used extensively and some very fine smock mills were built during the 19th century. It is not surprising therefore that, when in 1875, Mr George Jarvis, a young man who owned a carpenter's and wheelwright's shop in Bethersden, decided he needed power to drive his saws, he chose to erect a windmill. By this date, several of the established windmill sites were becoming non-operational due to the encroachment of residential properties. One such was a wind-powered sawmill at Sandgate, which Mr Jarvis purchased and re-erected in Bethersden. Coles-Finch recounts that Sandgate was not the original home of this mill; it originally stood at Pluckley near Ashford, where it was built as a sawmill for J. Padgham, a builder, being a smock mill with six sails. He later sold it to his brother who moved it to Great Chart, from where it was eventually moved to Sandgate. Rather surprisingly, Coles-Finch points out that there were only two six-sailed smock mills in Kent, both at Great Chart, from which it would appear that, as soon as the sawmill was sold to Mr Jarvis, a second sawmill was built on the same site, where it remained until demolished in 1938.

However, Mr Jarvis certainly used the six-sail mill to drive his carpenter's shop at Bethersden. But within a few years the expanding business required more power than this mill could provide. So in 1886 he bought a second mill, this time a smock corn mill – Dennison's Mill at Folkestone – which in turn had been moved previously to Folkestone from Penenden Heath. The newly acquired mill was duly re-erected at the Bethersden workshop, where it drove a saw mill. However, the millstones were retained and used by the local corn miller, as the need arose. The earlier six-sail smock mill may have continued in use as it was not pulled down until c.1896. The second mill was a weather-boarded smock mill with four single-sided patent sails and fantail, a very typical Kentish mill.

We also had wandering sawmills in Sussex. At Punnetts Town in 1866 a smock sawmill from Horam was moved and re-erected to provide power for the saw benches at a local timber yard. The smock was quite small with short patent sails, about 40 feet across, which Buckland suggests could only have produced 4hp at best. The spur wheel drove a lineshaft which took power to the main circular saw on the ground floor, with a belt drive to a smaller circular saw on the floor above. It is thought that the mill produced typical building materials, e.g. wainscot, floor boards and smaller joists. The mill was still working in 1925.

The 19th-century sawmills we have looked at so far were all standard windmills, of the design perfected in the relevant localities. Some were pure sawmills for the reduction of logs, some were workshops where further carpentry was carried out. During the second half of the century, a number of carpenters and joiners installed small wind engines on the roofs of their workshops, to drive wood-working machinery.

A wind-engine at Punnetts Town provides an excellent example. It was built in the 1880s to drive a saw and a drill in a workshop which produced staves for fattening coops (for livestock), and which continued in operation until c.1914. The device was essentially a wheel, approximately 12 feet in diameter with 14 arms or spokes. Around the rim were 70 fixed blades, i.e., they could not be feathered. The wind shaft was held in a weather-boarded frame, mounted on the flat roof of the workshop. Power was taken via an upright shaft, a belt drive and gears to the saw bench and drill. The device was winded by tail pole at roof level. The wind wheel must have had a modest power output and Buckland suggests it was probably a home-made version of the steel wind pumps which were beginning to appear at this date.

In Surrey, another home-made sawmill was built at Horsell Common in the 1880s by the Steer family, who were carpenters and builders. The structure comprised a rectangular weather-boarded shed, with the gable ends forming the longer sides. The roof ridge carried a penthouse along its entire length, the top of which was about 20 feet above ground level. The horizontal windshaft was mounted in the penthouse and carried four sails, comprised of longitudinal planks, which were hinged in the centre so that the sails could be either fully set or half set. Each side of the shed had a doorway and it is reported that there was a vertical timber shaft in the centre of the shed. The mill was used for sawing timber in the 1890s.

Farries and Mason conjecture that this may have been a fixed direction mill, but this seems unlikely. A photograph shows a gap between the bottom of the weather boarding and the ground and what we have here seems to be a version of the rather primitive paltrok type mill which one finds in Eastern Europe. The body would rest on timbers on the ground and be pivoted around the vertical timber pillar. Internally, the windshaft probably carried a belt pulley which drove the circular saw mounted on a frame at ground level. The log would be fed into the mill through one of the doors in the side wall, pass through the saw, and the cut timber would then be extracted through the door in the opposite wall.

A slightly more conventional wind sawmill was built in Surrey, at Buckland. The mill and workshop were built entirely of timber with weather board cladding, the mill having four patent sails and a fantail which were made by an engineer from Henfield in Sussex.

Away from the South East, in Lancashire a slightly larger version was built at Rimington. It stood on a three-storey brick workshop and comprised a skeletal tower with four single-sided patent sails mounted on an iron cross. Each sail had 21 shutters and a board along the leading edge which was slightly larger at the outer end than at the centre. The tip of each sail was connected by tie ropes. A striking rope hung at the rear of the tower which could be adjusted from a large stage at roof top level.

Also in Lancashire, at Freckleton, a joiner's workshop had a small windmill on its roof, which drove a circular saw and a lathe. The workshop was some 11 feet high to the ridge of the roof, on which a tower 8ft 6ins high was mounted. It had four common sails, each about eight feet long, set from a reefing stage at ridge level. The drive had three sets of gears, producing different ratios, which could be selected according to the speed at which the sails were turning.

At Holyhead on Anglesey, a tower mill built on a rocky crag above the yard of a building contractor, William Williams, provided power for the sawmill and joiner's shop by means of a drive shaft which ran the whole length of the building, from which belt drives were taken to various saws. At a later stage, steam power was added and the two worked in tandem until about 1916. The tower is shown on the firm's bill head as a tall tower mill with a stage and four sails.

Across the sea on the Isle of Man we have another example of a sawmill attached to a corn mill: Lezayne Mill at Ramsey, where the saw was used to cut timbers for a local ship builder. Also on the Isle of Man, at Kirk Michael, it appears a saw may have been added to a farm threshing mill.

The West Country had some areas which provided excellent wind power sites, particularly around the coast, and we have noted examples of wind power being

57 Rimington Joiner's Workshop, built during the 19th century.

used to de-water the non-ferrous metal mines in Cornwall. There are remains of a few corn windmills in the county but by and large the demand for corn mills was not great due to the comparatively sparse population, and the area had adequate water power sites which met most of the need. There is, however, a reference to a windmill on the quayside at St Ives, which may have been used in the 1860s by a wood carver and turner named James Cathorne. The evidence of this mill is somewhat ambiguous, being found in an inventory of 1883 which reads 'flour, saw and windmills'.

Lincolnshire was a county given over to arable farming, where there was very little timber grown. However, in 1853 a small brick tower mill, 33 feet high but fitted with five sails, was built at Kirton Lindsey, which drove two circular saws and one vertical saw. There are some points of interest concerning this mill. First, it was fitted with five sails, the recommendation of John Smeaton, a recommendation which during the 19th century was followed more than anywhere else in Lincolnshire. Secondly, at 33 feet it was very small but the village stands high on the Wolds to the west of the county, a useful site for wind power and, as no use would be found for the upper floors in a sawmill, it was sensibly only built to this height.

There were three corn mills in Lincolnshire which had a saw added, one being the magnificent eight-sail mill at Heckington and here again the saw was a vertical frame. The other two stood at Barrow on Humber, which had both a saw and a lathe, and one at Scawby.

It is not necessary to say anything further about the mill at Barrow, but the mill at Scawby was rather different. In 1822 *The Lincoln Rutland and Stamford Mercury* reported that '... a curiously constructed mill for breaking bones, grinding corn and sawing wood, the property of Robert Sutton, was blown down in a storm ...'. The combination of the description of a 'curiously constructed mill' and the name Robert Sutton suggests that this mill was probably fitted with Sutton's patent sails and windshaft (Patent No 2438, 13 August 1800). The patent, which has been eulogised over by Mr W.S. Hesleden, had three concepts. First the sails comprised longitudinal boards which could be twisted open and shut, controlled by a striking chain similar to Hooper's patent. In practice they would have been extremely heavy and the control gear rather weak. Secondly, to lighten the load on the neck bearing (and thus reduce friction), the brakewheel was moved to the rear of the wallower. Thirdly, again to reduce friction, he replaced the simple bush which carried the neck bearing of the windshaft with roller bearings. No doubt good in theory, in practice these ideas were doomed to failure.

Back in East Anglia we have an example which clearly demonstrates the versatility of the windmill. At Manea a tower mill with four sails was built *c.*1829, which drove a three-foot diameter circular saw, a lathe, a grindstone, a pump to de-water an adjacent clay pit, a set of brushes for cleaning boots and shoes, and apparatus for cleaning knives and forks. The mill must probably be regarded as a special case, being owned and operated by the Tidd Pratt commune, but nevertheless it was used for commercial purposes.

In this chapter we have looked at wind-powered sawmills used to provide power for a variety of woodworking premises. By this stage the astute reader may well be asking why, if wind power was so successful, did not the millwrights power their own workshops by wind? The answer is that in many cases their site was not suitable, but there is one firm who rescued the situation, Mr T.B. Hunt of Soham in Cambridgeshire. His workshop was powered by a windmill during the 19th century.

10

Supplying Water for Various Purposes

As was explained in the Preface, the use of wind power for land drainage schemes is outside the scope of the present study. Nevertheless, examples of the use of wind-powered pumps have been mentioned, for de-watering mines, quarries and brickworks. These uses have been to remove unwanted water but there are examples of water power being used to pump water in a more positive way, as part of a production process.

Salt Works
Salt has been an important commodity from well before the Norman Conquest, being used not only as a condiment but, probably more importantly in the days before the refrigerator, as a food preservative. Instead of buying salt by the pound weight, one reads of householders bringing home a barrow load of salt in the late autumn, in readiness for killing the family pig. Salt has been obtained from two basic sources, salt water and underground deposits, in the latter case either in the form of brine springs (as around Droitwich) or mining rock salt (as around Northwich and Winsford). Salt working has been an important part of the national economy, being a major export and a source of tax revenue to the government.

The earliest source was sea water and there are many places around the coast where salt works existed, the most important being in the South East (Dorset, Hampshire, Sussex and Kent), North Wales, Tyneside (which in the early 17th century produced more salt than anywhere else in England) and parts of Scotland. All these sea water operations were out of business by the mid-19th century when the market became dominated by the rock salt from mines in Cheshire.

The basic process of extracting salt from sea water, which varied only marginally from area to area, involved, first, the creation of a pond which would fill on the high tide and, as the tide receded, leave behind the raw material for the salt workers. From here the sea water was transferred to evaporating pans, if the contours allowed flowing by gravity along dikes, but in some areas, particularly Scotland, it had to be transferred by hand, using buckets. In some cases the water was pumped using wind engines. Once sufficient water had evaporated, the residual salt water was transferred to a boiling house where it was boiled in iron or copper pans.

There are several examples of salt works where wind engines were used to transfer the water from the evaporating pans on the south coast, e.g. at Lymington and Hayling Island. The mills were fairly slender structures, some 12 or 14 feet in height and it is arguable whether one regards these as skeletal smock mills or hollow post mills. They were fitted with four common sails and probably winded by vane. Each mill or wind engine drove a bucket pump. The total number is not known, but we do know that in 1749 the number of evaporating pans around the Solent was:

Lymington	149
Milford	50
Isle of Wight	42
Portsea	54

We have a map of Lymington, made in 1698, which shows 36 pans and five wind pumps, so we may assume a ratio of one pump to every seven or eight pans.

Another salt works on which we have information at Southwold in Suffolk, originally evaporating sea water. At some stage during the 19th century the works changed over to the use of rock salt. At first the material was transported by sea from Runcorn and Liverpool, later by train to Hull and then on by sea, but, after the Southwold Railway was opened in 1879, entirely by rail. Major Cooper visited the works shortly before they closed in 1894 and described the premises as follows:

> These works were situated at the head of the Saltworks Creek, up which the tide flowed into a well over which stood a small skeletal mill with canvas sail cloths, like little drainage mills, with open top pumps, and so common on the Suffolk Marshes. The water flowed from the pump along open troughs ... to the salt works and alongside to the Bath-house.

The windmill was an interesting structure. It comprised a square section timber frame, about 18 feet tall and three feet square, with a wide stage about

58 Windpump at Southwold Saltworks, Suffolk, built in the 1830s.

ten feet above ground level, and held upright by eight diagonal braces which met under the stage. The buck (or cap?) was a small open framework which carried four common sails, about six feet long, mounted on an iron cross. The mill was winded by a vane.

The next area of note was Tyneside, where, in 1748 there were some 200 pans (but this figure dropped to 20 in 1785). One of the difficulties faced by the salt producers was the demand for coal to heat the boiling pans. Several figures are quoted but it seems to have taken something like six tons of coal to produce one ton of salt, which accounts for the location of part of the industry on Tyneside. Indeed, further north, in Scotland, the salt works were frequently combined with a colliery under common ownership, non-commercial coal being used at the salt works.

An important salt works was laid out at St Monans in 1772/3, on the north shore of the Firth of Forth, which, as we have seen, was an area where wind power was used to pump water out of coal mines. The site of these works was investigated in some detail during the 1990s by the Tayside and Fife Archaeological Committee. It comprises a flattish rocky foreshore between the high and low water marks, then a strip of higher rocks, at the back of which is a 25-feet high raised beach. Thus in simple terms the site has three levels, the lower being covered at high tide and uncovered at low tide.

The salt works was laid out to maximise the opportunities presented by these three levels. The lowest level had two artificial rock pools which filled with water during the flood tide. Nine salt boiling pans were laid out in a shallow arc on the middle level, and on the top of the bank a wind engine was erected to drive a pump which lifted the water out of the rock pools into the boiling pans. A channel was cut into the rock which led the water from the pools towards the base of the wind engine tower, from where it was pumped into a header tank, from where in turn it flowed into the pans. Two wooden pipes were found in the channel, which indicates that the sea water was not conveyed about the site in open ducts, no doubt to prevent sea weed and other foreign matter getting into the system.

The wind pump was a sturdy battered tower of roughly-squared rubble stone, some 25 feet high and with an external diameter of 20 feet at the base. There are opposing doors on the east and west sides. A four-foot deep channel, cut into the ground on which the mills stands, passes from the centre of the ground floor, through a low opening in the wall of the tower immediately adjacent to the edge of the raised beach, and then continues down the slope across the central area out to the rock pools.

Unfortunately, there is no firm evidence of how the pump was connected to the wind engine. The report of the investigations into the site contains on the back cover a drawing showing a possible reconstruction of the works, in which two rocking beams extend from the base of the tower, with a linkage from an arch-head on each connected to a pump rod. This interpretation was no doubt based on the evidence of the pit extending into the base of the tower together with the drawing amongst the Rothes Manuscripts mentioned earlier (see page 86).

This arrangement requires a much stouter structure than one finds with English pumps and may offer one explanation of why the Scottish pumping engines were built so solidly.

The works were owned by the Newark Coal and Salt Work Company, established in 1771, who, as the name suggests, owned coal pits nearby. The site of the coal pits included the pit formerly owned by the Earl of Kellie, at which he had used wind power to de-water the workings. The site has been identified although there are no remains.

Several Scottish pumping windmills have been mentioned in the text, in connection with coal mines, quarries and the salterns. These are all now empty towers, so we have no archaeological evidence as to the internal machinery. However, there are the remains of a pumping mill, used for land drainage, which may give an indication as to the gearing in the various wind pumps mentioned so far. The mill is sited at Lonmay in Aberdeenshire, and comprises a battered stone tower. Around the top of the tower is a cast-iron curb with integral cast cogs around the outside, which probably indicates that the cap was winded by a fantail (although the Rothes drawing shows a tail pole). The windshaft is of cast iron but much shorter than common practice, the tail bearing being fixed to the cross beam which also carries the bearing for the upright shaft. A bevel gear wheel on the windshaft meshes with a similar wheel on the upright shaft, with an apparent ratio of one to one. The footstep bearing for the upright shaft is some three or four feet above ground level, above which is another bevel gear which drove a horizontal shaft (missing) which passed through the wall of the tower to the pump. This evidence is consistent with the drawing of the Rothes wind pump apart from, of course, the final drive to the pump. This difference can be accounted for because the Lonmay pump was designed for land drainage purposes.

There appears to have been no brake mechanism on the wind pump at Lonmay, an intriguing fact which resulted in a serious accident, causing the mill to be replaced by electric-powered pumps. Wind pumps, unlike corn mills, need to run round the clock to perform their function and one might expect them to be left running unattended. But in this vicinity, where strong gales are expected, some way of reducing the sail's area would be needed. The obvious answer in the late 18th century was the spring sail, invented in 1772 by the Scottish engineer Andrew Meikle, who was in business at East Lothian. Spring sails must be a possibility and the sails on the Rothes drawing appear to be consistent with this.

As we have seen, by the 1860s the saltern industry had come to an end, having being overtaken by the supply of rock salt from the mines in Cheshire. The raw material was transferred via the River Weaver to Liverpool where it was processed for sale (although substantial amounts of untreated rock salt were exported to Ireland for processing, thus avoiding the heavy excise duties).

The process used at Liverpool consisted of dissolving the rock salt in water tanks, emptying the solution into other tanks where it was clarified, and, finally, pumping it into the salt pans where it was boiled. Wind power was used to pump fresh water from wells.

59 Windmill at Saltworks, Dockside, Liverpool, built before 1754, taken from a very small pen and ink drawing in the Binn's Collection. The picture is labelled 'Herculaneum Potteries' but this seems to be an error, as the tall structure on the right is not a kiln but a glass cone at the adjacent glass works. The two premises can be readily identified from contemporary maps.

The earliest of the Liverpool salt works was owned by a Mr Blackburne and stood in the centre of the town, at Wapping on the south dock quay, now called the Salthouse Dock. It was visited by Angerstein in 1754 (he mis-spells the owner's name as Bletchford) and a diagram in his diary shows the windmill as a cylindrical tower mill, about 45 feet to the curb, with a domed cap, four common sails and winded by tail wheel. Angerstein shows the ground floor with a larger diameter than the tower, to form a plinth from which the sails could be set. He also records that internally the upright shaft reached down to ground level where a gear drove a crank shaft which worked four pump beams, which were not unlike the examples in Scotland. The gear connecting the upright shaft to the crank shaft could be disengaged as required. In the 1750s the premises were processing around nine tons of salt per week.

We also have a later sketch of this windmill, which is different from the diagram in Angerstein's diary in that it is shown as a standard type of Liverpool mill, having a tall battered tower with four common sails, chain wheel for winding and a stage at second-floor level. It is likely that Angerstein's drawing is somewhat stylised and that the later sketch is more accurate.

Around 1792 the mill was demolished when the adjacent dock was extended and Blackburne moved his works to Garston, a few miles to the south. Here he erected two windmills to pump water. Another salt works was opened still further south, the Dragon Saltworks at Hale, which was operated by Nicholas Ashton.

Canals

We have commented elsewhere in this study that considerable demand was placed on water resources as industrialisation developed during the 18th century. During that century a new demand emerged, arising from the developing canal network. The majority of canals were built to connect existing waterways by taking barges over a watershed, the journey up and down being achieved using locks. Each time a boat passed through a lock, a quantity of water in effect was removed from the summit level, i.e. the stretch of water between the top two locks on either side of the watershed, which had to be replenished from a reservoir or feeder which was at least as high as the summit level. In doing so they had to ensure that they did not interfere with the needs of any established water-powered mills, which in many cases were served by the canal. In some cases water had to be pumped from low level supplies, two examples occurring on the Kennet and Avon Canal, opened in 1810. The first was Claverton Pumping Station, where a large waterwheel (rated at 24hp) was used to lift water some 48 feet out of the River Avon, and the second was the well known Crofton Pumping Station, where two Boulton & Watt steam engines lifted water some 40 feet out of the nearby Wilton Water.

But not all proprietors had the funds for such expense and during the 18th century some used wind power. The Oxford Canal built two windmills, one at Hardwick Lock (1786), which was about half way up the climb northwards from Oxford, and a year later one at Hillmorton Locks towards the canal's northern end, both lifting water from adjacent streams. We have no details of the form of these wind pumps but we do know that one of the people concerned with the canal was sent to Cambridgeshire to study their use. It is most likely that the only wind pumps he would have seen in Cambridgeshire at that date were the land drainage pumps which lifted water using large paddle wheels (watermills working in reverse).

Another canal to use wind power was the Thames and Severn, opened in 1789. The summit level ran through an area called Thames Head, which, as the name suggests, is where many springs rise and combine to set the River Thames on its way to the sea. The company sank a borehole at the side of the canal and erected a wind pump to raise the water. The depth of the borehole was 54½ feet, the pump had a bore of 11 inches, and it is recorded that the engine threw up several tons of water every minute. This mill was an interesting structure, having a slim body, probably of timber, about 30 feet high and three or four feet square, with bracing about a third of the way up. A ladder led to a narrow stage just below the top of the body. There were six sails, about 10 to 12 feet long and it was probably winded by tail pole. The type of sail is not clear; they may have been common sails but it is quite possible that they were spring sails, which would make sense in the case of a mill which would be left to run night and day without close supervision. Although the wind pump provided the quantity of water predicted by the engineers, unfortunately their calculations proved wrong elsewhere, as a result of which the canal was chronically short of water. With experience gained from using the wind pump they decided to sink a second, larger well, but, to meet the much heavier demand, this pump was powered by a Boulton & Watt engine.

Finally, the Wey and Arun Canal, which was built to link these two rivers in an attempt to provide an inland route between London and the South Coast. Again the water supply, a reservoir feeding the summit level, proved to be inadequate, even after it was deepened. The company sought advice from George Rennie (son of John Rennie) who came up with an interesting solution, a version of the water-returning engine. He suggested that two wind pumps should be built, at the top two locks on the northern descent to the River Wey, to pump water back from below the lock to the pound above it. The first, erected at the top lock (subsequently named Cranley Mill), was completed in 1833 at a cost of £285. It was a smock mill on a brick foundation, some 16 feet high and 12 feet wide. It drove two 12-inch pumps which raised 350 gallons a height of seven feet per minute. Thus, to return the water used when a boat passed through the lock back to the summit level would take 70 minutes. The mill was adequate for this lock but the second, at the next lock down, needed to be a more powerful affair. Completed in 1834 at a total cost of £670, it stood 24 feet high on a

60 Wind pump built in the 1780s at Thames Head on the Thames and Severn Canal to raise water from a well into the canal.

base 26 feet in diameter. It had four shuttered sails (40 shutters in each), 20 feet long and nine feet wide. The cap was winded by fantail. These mills continued in use for some 20 years by which time they were worn out and offered for sale.

Public Water Supply

The advent of schemes to provide water to domestic properties, and thus relieve the housewife of the need to visit the village pump each day, might have made the windmill an economic choice. In fact the earliest and best known example seems to have been singularly unsuccessful. In 1613 the first major scheme to bring fresh water into London had been completed, the water being delivered to the round pond in Islington, known as River Head. In 1708 a higher level reservoir had to be built, 33 feet above the level of the original pond, to enable a supply to be fed to additional properties. To lift the water a wind-powered pump was used, which was quite an impressive piece of architecture. It comprised a battered brick tower, probably some 40 feet high, with a stage at first-floor level. The first and second floors had large oval shaped windows and the cap was domed with an impressive ball finial. Defoe recounts that it had six sails but these had gone by his visit in the 1720s, at which date the power was provided by 'many horses constantly working'. It continued in this fashion until replaced by a steam engine designed by Smeaton.

A contemporary example which had some success was built at King's Lynn in *c.*1698. Originally the town's water supply had been obtained from a stream from

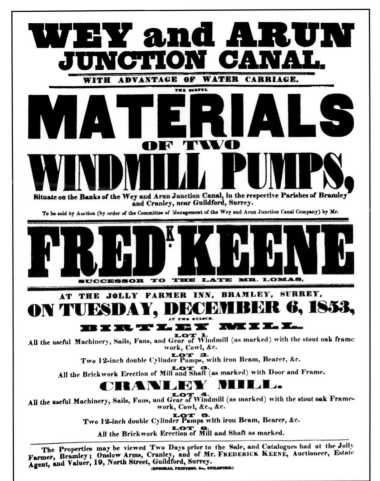

WEY and ARUN JUNCTION CANAL.

WITH ADVANTAGE OF WATER CARRIAGE.

THE USEFUL

MATERIALS

OF TWO

WINDMILL PUMPS,

Situate on the Banks of the Wey and Arun Junction Canal, in the respective Parishes of Bramley and Cranley, near Guildford, Surrey.

To be sold by Auction (by order of the Committee of Management of the Wey and Arun Junction Canal Company) by Mr.

FREDᴷ KEENE

SUCCESSOR TO THE LATE MR. LOMAS,

AT THE JOLLY FARMER INN, BRAMLEY, SURREY,

ON TUESDAY, DECEMBER 6, 1853,

AT TWO O'CLOCK.

BIRTLEY MILL.

LOT 1.
All the useful Machinery, Sails, Fans, and Gear of Windmill (as marked) with the stout oak frame work, Cowl, &c.

LOT 2.
Two 12-inch double Cylinder Pumps, with iron Beam, Bearer, &c.

LOT 3.
All the Brickwork Erection of Mill and Shaft (as marked) with Door and Frame.

CRANLEY MILL.

LOT 4.
All the useful Machinery, Sails, Fans, and Gear of Windmill (as marked) with the stout oak Framework, Cowl, &c., &c.

LOT 5.
Two 12-inch double Cylinder Pumps with iron Beam, Bearer, &c.

LOT 6.
All the Brickwork Erection of Mill and Shaft as marked.

The Properties may be viewed Two Days prior to the Sale, and Catalogues had at the Jolly Farmer, Bramley; Onslow Arms, Cranley, and of Mr. FREDERICK KEENE, Auctioneer, Estate Agent, and Valuer, 19, North Street, Guildford, Surrey.

(RUSSELL, PRINTERS, &c., GUILDFORD.)

61 Handbill for the sale of two windpumps, built in 1833 and 1834, used on the Wey and Arun Canal to return water from below two locks to the pound above them.

where it was led around the town in timber pipes, flowing under gravity. But in 1682 some alterations were made to the dike from which the supply was obtained and a windmill was erected to lift the water some 30 or 40 feet up into a wooden tank, located in a former tower of the town wall. This continued in use for some 80 years, until 1780, when as Hillen writes: 'The old water engine was found to be in a hopeless condition, and as the ingenuity of the Lynn machinists was of no avail, a new engine was obtained.'

The new engine was a Newcomen steam engine. Little is known of the windmill but the 'Prospect of the Town' dated 1741 shows what appears to be a smock mill in the vicinity of the water tower marked on a map of 1846 and, having regard to the fact that by the date this mill was built the town had already acquired two Dutch-style oil smock mills, the windmill marked on the 1741 'prospect' may be the mill driving the water engine.

As new water supply schemes were introduced during the 19th century into expanding towns and cities, the power demands would have outstripped the capacity of a single windmill; water supply was an industry where the beam pumping engine came into its own. But in the case of small villages, the wind pump was able to meet the need.

An interesting example occurred at Copton near Faversham in Kent, where, in 1863, the Faversham Water Company built a wind pump to draw water into a reservoir from a well beneath the station. It was rated at 15hp and is claimed to have pumped 10,000 gallons per hour. The mill continued in use until 1893.

The best known example still stands, at Thorpeness in Suffolk, where a post corn mill, moved from Aldringham in 1922, was re-erected. In doing so the upright post was bored out to take a pumping rod, which pumped water from a well to a nearby water tower. The tower supplied water to houses on the Thorpeness estate. In a steady wind the mill could lift 1,800 gallons per hour and continued in use until about 1940.

In fact, this mill replaced an iron wind pump of the sort produced from the 1880s onwards, particularly by the well known supplier John Wallis Titt. One of this firm's wind pumps, used to supply water to nearby properties at Crux Easton in Hampshire, has recently been restored. A large number of these pumps were erected, including a very attractive example at Southport.

Water for Alcoholic Beverages

Water, whilst wholesome and a necessity for life, is not the most exciting drink. There are examples of wind power being used for the production of alcoholic drinks.

The first occurred at Haigh near Wigan, where wind power was used at a brewery to pump water from a well. It comprised a slender tower, some nine feet in diameter at the base, fitted with four roller sails, controlled from a cast-iron stage. A small dome-shaped cap had an iron frame. The mill still stands, although without most of its original features.

The second example was in Dover where the Buckland Breweries had a pumping mill until the 1860s. The mill was typical of the Kentish smock mill, with four single-sided sails and winded by fantail. The brick base was larger than the standard in the area, being a rectangular two-storey structure.

The third and earliest example occurred in Scotland where the Society of Brewers used a wind engine to pump water from the Burgh Loch. It had been demolished by 1768 and the site has now been built over by the University.

The remaining two are in Scotland, the first at Kirkcudbright, where it is thought to have driven, surprisingly, a cider mill. The design is unusual, being a cylindrical tower some 28 feet high and a little over 19 feet in diameter at the base. It is built of rubble stone but with five projecting courses of dressed sandstone. The tower forms part of a large complex of buildings, one of which it adjoins. Where it connects to this building there is a rectangular projection which extends some two and a half feet and continues up above the top some six feet. The purpose of this projection is a mystery.

The final mill was at the Glenugie Distillery. Built of coursed granite, it was one of the taller Scottish mills, being 46 feet to the curb with a diameter at the base of 18 feet. The empty towers of these last two mills still stand.

11

Some Other Uses

Today we have a renewed interest in the use of wind power to produce electricity. It is not intended to rehearse the arguments for and against this modern practice but to point out that it is far from a new phenomenon. There have been previous examples.

Indeed, the first was as early as 1887 when Professor James Blyth of Glasgow erected a horizontal windmill to generate electricity. The machine developed 4hp and he suggested that individual electric aerogenerators (as they are now called) would be ideal in isolated places. He suggested that wind power could be used at lighthouses, citing two examples at Cap de la Hero near La Havre, and to provide lighting in private country houses. His great-granddaughter recounts that he offered to light the village of Marykirk but the villagers were suspicious of the newfangled invention and turned him down. Only one commercial example was erected, to light Sunnyside Asylum near Montrose. His original generator was demolished in 1906.

Another example was erected at St Margaret's Bay, Kent, in 1928 for Sir William Beardsworth. The millwrights were Holman Brothers and the design was the standard Kentish smock mill, with four double patent sails and upright fantail. The main variation from the standard external appearance is the area underneath

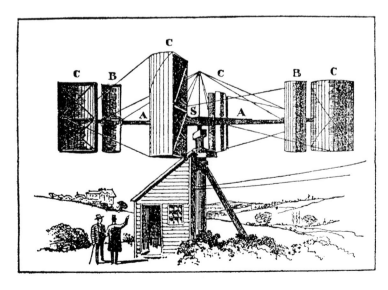

62 Horizontal windmill, built in 1887 at Marykirk in Scotland, to generate electricity.

the stage, which has been filled in to provide living accommodation. It ceased to function in 1939 and the generator has since been removed but the remainder of the structure still stands, in working order.

The issue of providing power in isolated places leads us into agriculture. The Orkney Islands are probably as isolated as one can get in Britain, but the farmers have needed power to crush and thresh grain, like any other farmer, and there were very limited opportunities for water power. A particular type of post mill, the turret mill, was used for grain milling, which is certainly outside the scope of this work, but an interesting type of threshing mill was developed in the late 19th century, which was particularly suited to an area of high winds. Ten of these threshing mills have been identified by the SIAM, the most complete being at Sanquhar Farm on Westray, which continued in use until 1950.

The mill is built onto the side of the barn and comprises two flagstone-capped rectangular columns, some 11 feet high, each a little over two feet wide and about 1ft 10ins apart. They support a 20-inch hollow wooden centre post which extends some eight feet above the top of the columns. The hollow post carries a two-inch diameter wrought iron upright shaft, with a casting at the top which carries the short windshaft, from which the drive is transmitted by two bevel gearwheels. The front end of the windshaft has a cast-iron hub which carried six jib sails, their overall diameter being some 10½ feet.

In England, during the 19th century, the model farm was emerging. It had a carefully planned layout and power to drive various items of machinery in the farm buildings. The largest used steam power in the form of the traction engine but some used water power and, in a number of cases, wind power. A surviving example is at Halstead House farm, Tilton on the Hill, in Leicestershire. Here a two-storey barn was powered by wind. The windmill was built into the centre of the barn and comprised four large inclined timbers which supported the wind engine, which has now gone. The engine was probably of the type being mass-produced by Bury and Pollard, which had up to eight small sails mounted on a lattice frame. The firm's advertisements indicate that they had several versions, with power ratings ranging from as little as a half-horse power up to 12 horse power.

Agricultural uses are on the border of the present study, but they have been given a brief mention to show the versatility of the windmill and, with the examples of the threshing mills on the Orkneys, to give a pointer to the way in which wind power may be used beneficially today to generate electricity.

Finally, it must be accepted that there were some cases where wind power was tried, but it didn't work.

The first was spotted by Angerstein somewhere in the Wolverhampton area, where he visited a forge making gun barrels belonging to a Mr Willits. He explains that the boring machine was powered by a water wheel but that the works were occasionally stopped due to lack of water. To overcome this difficulty, Willits had built what Angerstein describes as a Dutch windmill of brick, which was said to have cost a large sum of money. A sketch by Angerstein of the premises shows a small group of sheds, with what must be an undershot water wheel fed from an adjacent pond. Towering above the sheds is a large conical tower mill wedged in between the sheds and the pond.

He then goes on to say that

> ... it had never been used because the English are not so familiar with windmills and that Willits was prepared to spend a considerable sum of money to learn a way of taking in the sails without stopping the mill, because the stopping is very inconvenient and also dangerous in view of the position of the mill just above the water ...

There are a number of interesting points in this statement. When he was writing, in 1754, English millwrighting does not seem to have had a very good reputation! Also, here we have an industrialist who was finding the lack of self-regulation of windmill sails a clear problem. Finally, it is hardly surprising that setting the sails was dangerous, because the mill was so close to the mill pond, which says something about Mr Willits and possibly the millwright he engaged, if any.

The second example of a windmill which failed to work was another attempt to build a horizontal mill, at Redditch. It was built c.1780, the sails being located inside a rectangular tower, with slits in the brickwork to admit the wind. The windmill was to be used to drive machinery for making needles, a speciality of the area, but the arrangement did not work and the structure was converted to artisan dwellings.

Thirdly we have a corn mill which by the 1830s was out of use and the machinery had been removed. This is a little early for a windmill to close and the reason for it would be interesting. However, the empty tower was put to good use by William Gossage, the well known alkali manufacturer. The effluent from the alkali manufacturing process contained hydrochloric acid which was disposed off by venting it to the air, with predictable consequences for the surrounding flora and fauna. Gossage devised a method of filtering the effluent, which he tested by packing the empty tower with brushwood and venting the effluent into the structure. The arrangement proved a success and Gossage patented the system in 1836. Thereafter, purpose-built structures were used for the process. The exact site of the tower has not be ascertained but it is believed to have been at Stoke Prior in Worcestershire.

12

Analysis and Comment

Having completed an account of the various applications of wind power, it is now possible to attempt an assessment of its contribution to the industrial activity of the time. A simple head count, compared with the other contemporary sources of power, might produce one result but it would tell us nothing about the quality of such contribution. The better approach is to ask why wind power was used in a particular situation and attempt a guess, for this is all it can be after such a lapse of time, as to what it enabled particular industrialists to achieve.

The majority of the examples included in this study were built during the 18th and 19th centuries, which period includes the phenomenon generally referred to as the industrial revolution. This was clearly an event of prime importance to the country, which makes it surprising that historians are far from agreed as to what it was and when it happened. An eminent early writer defined the period as 1760 to 1830, but later writers tend to go for a later start date. There is also disagreement as to its end date; some even maintain that it is still taking place (which makes it a long revolution). As to what it was, this can vary according to the point of view of the writer. Landscape historians see it as the period during which industry changed from being based on water power to being based on steam power. The effect of this, they would say, is that during the former period there was very little change in the natural landscape apart from a few sooty deposits from those concerns which used coal directly, and a few spoil heaps. But the latter period resulted in urban sprawl in the valley bottoms and tightly packed unhealthy housing conditions, removing nature's greenery in the process. The social historian would interpret these changes by reference to their effect on people's lives.

As wind power is an essential part of the history of technology, we could simply take the approach of the historian of technology. He might say that it was the period during which there was a sudden outburst of mechanical ingenuity and inventive genius, when practical men produced new devices to enable tasks to be performed more quickly, more conveniently and more economically. But the period is hardly unique so far as new inventions are concerned; the application of water power to drive mills was the first of a long line of ingenious devices, commencing back in classical times. If one takes the patent list as a measure, we see that, of the 13,000 patents granted between 1630 and 1850, well over half were not granted until after 1830. The annual rate did start to rise in the 1780s but there was hardly an explosion in the 18th century. The rate of increase showed a number of identifiable peaks, but Professor Ashton has pointed out that '… at each of the peaks the rate of interest [for borrowing money] was below the prevailing level and that at each of them expectations of profit were running high.'

Professor Ashton was, of course, the Professor of Economic History at London University. It seems to the author that the significant description of the industrial revolution lies with the economic historians, who regard it as the period when there was a coming together for the first time of several factors – an expanding market (at home and abroad), the availability of capital, the right political and legal environment, and, probably most important of all, the existence of entrepreneurs who had the ability and the drive to put capital to work and maximise the return to investors, i.e. to make a good profit.

Consequently, when we try to analyse the contribution of wind power to industry, we are investigating how the windmill enabled the industrialist to make his profit.

It is useful at this point to recapitulate the options available to industrialists who wanted some form of mechanical power during the first half of the 18th century. The most effective and oldest source was water power, which by this date was being used extensively in Britain, not only to grind grain but also for fulling, paper making, iron forges, smelting iron and sharpening edge tools. The total number of water power sites is not known but it was obviously a large figure, so much so that by the 18th century, water-powered sites in practical locations were at a premium. Elsewhere, the horse mill was used, a particular application being for pumping and winding at mines. Although the horse mill provided very little power and had a comparatively low capital cost, they were expensive to run, horses required to be fed whether or not they were at work, and manpower was needed to supervise the operation and take care of the animals. Wind power was available but until the late 16th century had been restricted to grain milling. The usual windmill at that date was the post mill, a cumbersome machine which was demanding of the operator. Finally came steam power, first in the form of the Savery engine and, from 1712, the Newcomen engine, both designed for the specific purpose of pumping water. But it was not until the Boulton & Watt rotary engine appeared in the 1780s that a practical steam engine became available for driving machinery. However, this was expensive both to build and to operate, the latter cost increasing proportionally to the distance from the nearest coal mine.

The date 1800 was something of a watershed in the evolution of power, being the date when the Boulton & Watt patent for their steam engine expired and the brakes came off the development of steam power. Not surprisingly, this had an effect on the application of other power sources, including wind power, and for this reason it is useful to look at the present subject in two parts. First, the period up to 1800 (or thereabouts) and, secondly, the subsequent period.

During the period up to 1800, the significant users of wind power in England and Wales were the oil seed crushers, the non-ferrous metal industries (both mining and subsequent activities), the potters, the producers of paint pigment and the producers of snuff, with a little foray into paper making.

The first oil mills in England were established to crush various seeds, particularly rape, hemp and line, produced by the home farmers, mainly in the eastern counties. These were areas where no effective water power was available, so the early seed merchants had to rely on horse-driven mills. Seed crushing produced two basic commodities, oil and cakes. The woollen textile industry provided a ready market for the oil, but the cake had little economic value in England, being exported to Northern Europe where it was used as cattle feed. Surplus seed was similarly exported. In these circumstances it is hardly surprising that the merchants in the east coast ports were the principal players in this export trade. Thus we learn of seed crushing in King's Lynn, Wisbech, Spalding, Boston, Gainsborough, Hull and London.

Seed production increased dramatically in the 17th century when land reclamation schemes were being promoted in the Fens and elsewhere and the merchants needed more power to cope with the increased demand. When in 1638 a seed merchant in King's Lynn erected a Dutch built wind-powered seed crushing mill, he chose a power source less expensive to operate than a horse mill. The capital cost would have been greater but capital was readily available and the repayment costs would have been met by increased output. In the light of contemporary experiences with home-built windmills in King's Lynn, it was hardly surprising that the merchant turned to a Dutch millwright to execute the work.

The windmill proved successful as, after a short pause during the Civil War, a second Dutch-style oil mill was built in King's Lynn, in 1680, and eventually wind power was adopted by the major oil merchants in all the ports mentioned above.

By the start of the 18th century, the nature of the industry had changed considerably. Most seed was being imported (from Northern Europe) and the value of the residual cake as a cattle food had been recognised in England. The ports where the seed crushing industry had become established were the very ports through which the foreign seed was being imported. Unfortunately, during the 18th century the Fenland ports ran into difficulties, as navigation in the Wash became more problematical, only King's Lynn surviving for any length of time. During the century, colonial expansion introduced new seed to the industry, from America, Africa and India, which resulted in Liverpool entering the field. Liverpool had a limited amount of water power available but this was already fully occupied, so here again wind power was used. As a result during the 19th century the main seed crushing ports were London, Liverpool and Hull, together with inland ports served by the Humber, namely, Gainsborough and Leeds. Without the availability of wind power one might ask whether the English merchants would have been able to meet the rapidly growing demand for oil. If not, would the trade have moved elsewhere, for example, to the seed producing areas on the continent?

So, why did these merchants use wind power and what did it achieve? The answer to the first question is simple – they had no option; the ports were the preferred location in which to establish their businesses and wind power was the only mechanical power available. The second part of the question is more difficult but one might conclude that the availability of efficient wind-powered seed crushing plant enabled the merchants to establish well-founded profitable concerns which were well placed to expand into the 19th century. When steam power became a more economic option, these firms took advantage of the new power source but this does not in any way detract from the basic fact that it was wind power which enabled the merchants to establish their concerns in the first place. These firms made a positive contribution to the economic well-being of the relevant towns. For example, in the case of Hull, as the town developed, it also encouraged the creation of engineering companies specialising in the production of seed crushing machinery together with supporting industries, which interacted well with other engineering-based industries in the town. In time, the town became the major producer of seed crushing machinery, with the firm of Rose Downs and Thompson becoming world-famous in this field. As oil is a basic ingredient of paint, the manufacture of this product also became an important industry.

During the 18th century some of the newly emerging industries relied entirely on the craft skills of their employees for most of their operations but had a need for power for a part of the process, usually crushing or mixing materials. The first example is found in the Staffordshire ceramics industry, more particularly in the small town of Burslem where the Wedgwood family were at the forefront of the English effort to produce white wares. Unfortunately, Burslem was the least favoured of the Six Towns in respect of water-powered sites, so in 1750 Brindley built a windmill in the village to grind flint, which was successful and used by local potters, including the Wedgwoods.

When Josiah Wedgwood opened his new pottery at Etruria, in 1769, he changed working practices to the extent that workers carried out a particular part of the manufacture only, they did not produce the article from start to finish. But they were still craftsmen, working manually. The siting of the factory was important, being in an area where coal was readily available and next to the proposed canal, which would transport raw materials in and completed goods out. It was also nearer to Hanley, where water power was available and where Wedgwood rented and converted a watermill to grind his flint. But power was needed to crush and mix materials at the factory and in 1774 Wedgwood erected a windmill to perform this task. He did give some consideration to using steam power but at this date rotary motion was still problematical and, having had the experience of using Brindley's wind-powered flint mill at Burslem, built some 20 years earlier, he chose the more economic option. As the business expanded, he did add a steam engine to drive some of the machinery but found the windmill useful for crushing and mixing experimental materials. Wedgwood's lead was followed by another potter, Enoch Wood, who used wind power to crush and mix materials at his pottery in Burslem well into the 1780s.

A similar situation occurred at Leeds Pottery, built by the Green Brothers during the 1760s. Here local clays were used and coal was obtained from the nearby Middleton Colliery. So important was the supply of coal to the siting of the mill that the mill was built straddling the wooden wagonway from the colliery to the staithes (opened in 1758). This site could not have been economical without the use of wind power.

If we now turn to the production of white and red lead, Walker established his first lead factory at Elswick in Newcastle, a site chosen because of the availability of local coal and convenient for obtaining lead ore from the mines in the Pennines to the west. Using the Dutch process, the conversion of metallic lead to the oxide took about 10 to 12 weeks, of which only three weeks might be required for the crushing operation, for which Walker used wind power. The windmill obviously proved successful and enabled the company to open a second factory in London and a third at Derby without having to seek out a water-powered site.

A similar situation arose in Liverpool, where a very limited amount of water power was available but by the mid-18th century these sites were fully occupied. The merchants producing paint (oil and colour) chose to use the well established windmill to treat their raw materials.

Thus, as far as these emerging industries were concerned, a limited amount of water power was available in the vicinity of the chosen sites but it was all fully committed. The factory owners could have tried to buy suitable water mills but power was only needed for a small part of their operation and it would have been uneconomic to go to such expense. Wind power was available which could satisfy the power demand and was used by these concerns during their formative years.

The same considerations must have faced merchants in Bristol who wanted to start producing snuff. There was considerable competition for the water-powered sites in the area, forcing the snuff makers who wanted to use water power well out of the town. Some decided to use wind power which enabled them to operate nearer to the town centre. But in any event a lot of snuff can be produced by one man with a modest amount of power.

Returning to non-ferrous metals, when William Champion and Charles Roe established their brass works at Warmley and Macclesfield respectively, they did have access to water power but not in sufficient quantity. At Warmley, Champion had installed a water-returning engine using a Newcomen-type engine, which was proving to be inadequate, so for extra power he erected a wind engine. At Macclesfield, Roe used wind power for ore crushing, all his available water power being taken up by machinery producing finished goods. Here we have wind power supporting an inadequate water power site. At Warmley the windmill was a far more economical option than a second Newcomen engine and similarly at Macclesfield where no steam power was used.

The concept of supporting inadequate water power occurred in London across a range of industries. By the end of the 18th century, London was a densely populated area, whose inhabitants demanded a plethora of goods for their convenience and pleasures. A number of tributaries to the Thames offered water power within practical reach of the City, but these were all occupied. Kenneth

Farries lists some 650 water mill sites, most providing flour and animal feed, but there was also a large demand for paper, with other mills providing snuff, dressed leather, silks and, uniquely, polished diamonds, which a contributor to *The Ambulator* observed ran at considerably less expense than previously when they were driven by horses or men. Two of these water-powered mills were used to crush wood for paint dyes. When extra power was required to increase output, windmills were added at each site in preference to the more expensive options of steam or horse power.

So, during the 18th century, wind power was used by industrialists in essentially three sets of circumstances:

1. Where no water power was available;
2. Where water power was available but the sites were fully occupied and, as the power was needed for only a small part of the operation, it was more economic to use wind power than to buy out an existing user;
3. Where water power was available and used by a factory owner but the available power was insufficient for his needs.

In the 1790s, steam power had become a practical proposition. We have seen in Hull what might have been an attempt to convince industrialists that wind power was a better option than steam, with the erection of the first wind-powered paper mill. It was certainly a successful venture in itself and, if it was intended as a competitor to steam power, it was successful in the short term. But during the 19th century those manufacturers who had established their businesses using wind power were starting to expand and, as they did so, their power requirements outstripped the twenty or so horse power which the windmill could provide. Their requirements changed in other respects. The potters introduced mechanisation, e.g. the jolly, so the power requirements were for more than the crushing of raw materials. Eventually, manufacturers introduced shift working, with employees having to work to a prearranged timetable, a system which the windmill could not hope to satisfy due to the vagaries of the wind, even if its power output was sufficient.

Nevertheless, whilst the steam engine had been developing, major improvements had been made to the windmill. Tall tower mills were becoming common, iron gearing was much more reliable, the fantail relieved the operator from having to keep an eye on the wind. The roller sail and the spring sail produced a reasonably constant speed, a facility which was substantially improved when in 1807 the patent sail combined these two features. At this point the English windmill became an efficient and easy-to-use engine.

Consequently, during the 19th century, wind power was still attractive to industrialists where power was needed for a small part of a larger operation. Whiting mills were erected at several chalk quarries, where the main product was chalk for civil engineering. The quarries naturally occurred along the limestone outcrops which ran through East Yorkshire, Lincolnshire, parts of East Anglia and down into Hampshire, all areas within the windmill zone, and some ten windmills were built between 1812 and 1838 for this purpose.

Similarly at the tanneries, of which there must have been several hundred in market towns spread across the country. Here again, wind power was used, mainly in the eastern counties, but also in good wind power areas such as the Cumberland coast at Wigton and Cockermouth, the Welsh coast at Aberystwyth, and at Wellington near Taunton in Somerset.

Further examples occurred at brickworks, in Anglesey, Newcastle, and Hornsea on the Yorkshire coast, where wind power was used to crush clay. This is a minute proportion of the literally thousands of small brickyards which were opened to meet the massive increase in house building. In many cases the brick maker would simply dig up the nearest field he could get his hands on, taking out a fairly shallow layer of clay, with the spreading development soon engulfing the workings, as happened in Newcastle. Many of these concerns were by nature short-lived and did not justify the capital expense of using wind power to drive crushing plant. But wind power did prove extremely useful, one might say vital, to the prosperity of the brickmaker. Today, the pits of former brick works can be seen, full of water. Whilst a boon for today's anglers, keeping clay pits free from water was a serious problem when one wanted to extract the clay. There are numerous examples of small windmills being used to drive simple bucket pumps to perform this function. Some were small tower mills but many were simple hollow post mills, the latter being extremely cheap and easy to build, with the added advantage that they could be quite easily moved about the site, if required. There must be many cases where claypits could not have been dug economically without the use of wind power.

Another industry which blossomed during the building boom were the timber merchants. We have seen that, in the 17th century, the sawyers were keen to prevent the installation of mechanical sawing but, with the invention of the circular saw, they were unable, or chose not, to prevent its spread, and there must have been hundreds of small sawmills across the country. Some still used the saw frame, e.g. the water-powered sawmills Gunton (*c*.1820) and Powys (*c*.1830) but the circular saw was a much simpler machine and could easily be installed in either a wind or watermill. The main area for wind-powered sawmills was again the eastern counties, with a particularly large group around Norwich. One writer has made the point that, apart from Cornwall, Norfolk was the county furthest from any coal mine!

The improvements made to windmill design also enabled comparatively small wind engines to be built. There were several examples of small joiners' workshops where a wind engine (providing probably no more than 5hp) was erected on the roof, to drive not only saws but in some cases lathes or drills. There are also many cases where a wind corn mill (and indeed some water corn mills) had a saw bench added, some as late as the 1850s. Thus we have a very economic source of power available to small businesses – family concerns employing perhaps only a handful of men.

The possibility of adding other plant to corn mills was taken up in Oxfordshire, when a deposit of ochre was discovered, the plant being used to crush the ochre for use as a paint pigment. Thus, the windmill in these cases provided power for the ochre producer at minimal cost whilst at the same time no doubt providing welcome additional income for the corn miller at a time when he was beginning to feel the effect of competition from the larger town mills.

In some cases industrialists simply took over an existing corn mill for their operation, e.g. the coprolite works at Bassingbourn, the emery grinding mill at St Helens and more recently the corn mill at Werringham used in connection with the production of coal bricks. In one case, corn mills in the Isle of Axholme may well have been used to grind gypsum, without any alteration to the mill, the stones simply being cleaned out before milling the next batch of grain.

In all these cases the windmill contributed to the output of the industrialist at an economic cost.

So, to summarise the position during the 19th century, the windmill was used by industrialists in the following circumstances:

1. Where power was only required for a small part of the operation;
2. Where small family concerns had a need for a modest amount of power, particularly in rural areas;
3. Where existing corn mills had sufficient capacity to install additional non-milling plant. And, in one case at least, existing millstones may have been used to support an industrial operation (i.e. gypsum).

Finally, Professor Jennifer Tann has suggested one other way in which wind power contributed to the industrial viability of the nation. In some regions, existing water-powered corn mills were being converted to alternative industrial uses. She cites the Weald in Kent and Sussex where water-powered sites were converted to forges and iron rolling and slitting mills, in Lancashire and Cheshire where water corn mills were converted to cotton textiles, and in Yorkshire to woollen textile mills. This left an immediate shortfall in flour production, which must surely have been one cause of the increase in numbers of wind-powered corn mills built during the 18th century. It is difficult to pinpoint specific examples, particularly as an increase in demand also arose from the general increase in population which occurred in the areas where these industries were established.

Broadly speaking, the main uses of industrial wind power can be grouped either side of the rough dividing date of 1800. For example, the oil mills were mainly built during the period up to say 1810, whereas the sawmills, whiting mills and oak bark mills were mainly built in the 19th century. But there is one use which continued throughout the entire period, namely the use of wind power to pump water. It must be recognised that, in some cases, such uses had only a short life, being superseded by the Newcomen engine. Nevertheless, wind power was particularly important to the brickmakers, the salt producers and in a few cases to the financially hard-pressed canal, mines and quarry proprietors. Not only did these uses persist throughout the entire period, they also covered the whole country, examples occurring from John O'Groats to Lands End.

As a result of this spread of time and location, the wind pump appeared in a wide variety of forms. For example, in Scotland they were substantial tower mills, externally not much different from the local corn mills, whereas in the clay pits of Lincolnshire and East Yorkshire the tower mills were much smaller structures and in this region we also find small hollow post mills.

The Scottish examples were no doubt designed to withstand the severe gales experienced in that region, but the wind pump has no internal machinery – all that is needed is some structure to hold the wind engine at a suitable height above the pump, which in most cases is below ground level. As a result millwrights recognised that the 'tower' could be reduced to a minimum width, for example to a simple timber frame as at the salterns at Lymington and Southwold, or the pump at Thames Head on the Thames and Severn canal. Here the structure was basically a hollow post with a simple framework to hold the wind engine, often without any cover. Although these are usually classified as hollow post mills, one might almost regard them as slender tower mills with a tiny cap. However they are described, it must be recognised that they were comparatively inexpensive structures and ideally suited to the purpose for which they were intended.

During the 19th century this concept was adopted in America with the emergence of the factory-produced prefabricated iron wind engine which could be mounted on an open steel frame, although early examples, e.g. the fuller's earth mine at Odd Down, had a timber frame. This idea was taken up by English engineering firms, e.g. John Wallis Titt, Wakes and Lamb, and, whereas initially some quite large structures were built, this type of wind pump became popular in its ubiquitous smaller form and was used by farmers until comparatively recent times.

Having attempted an assessment of the value of wind power to Britain's industrialists, it is perhaps pertinent to look at the reverse side of the coin. Did the intervention of the industrialists produce any benefits for the corn millers, who had been using wind power since the late 12th century. Up to the start of the 18th century the predominant windmill used to grind corn was the post mill, with a few small cylindrical stone tower mills. Until the early 1600s, both of these mill types had been small structures with only one pair of millstones. By the end of the 19th century the wind-powered corn mill was a very different affair.

To make such an assessment, it is first necessary to choose a mill which might be described as the ultimate in English wind-powered corn mill design. There is room for argument over such a choice, but for the purpose of this exercise it is proposed to look at Sibsey Trader Mill in Lincolnshire. This is not an entirely arbitrary decision; Sibsey Trader Mill was one of the last windmills to be built (1877) and is one of the four windmills Rex Wailes selected to examine in detail in his definitive book on the technology of the English windmill. It continued in operation until 1954, following which it was taken over by the Department of the Environment for preservation.

Sibsey Trader Mill is a brick tower mill of six floors with an ogee cap, reaching a little over 74 feet above ground level. It has six double-sided patent sails and an upright gallows fantail. The windshaft, upright shaft and gears are of cast iron. There were four pairs of millstones at third-floor level, originally two pairs of French stones and two pairs of grey stones.

These features are radically different from the timber postmill of earlier times and, if one considers the origin of these differences, we find an interesting scenario. The concept of the tall tower mill has its origins in the two Dutch oil mills built in King's Lynn, followed by the tall brick tower oil mill built for Joseph Pease in Hull by Dutch millwrights. The use of cast iron was promoted by John Smeaton and first applied to a wind-powered oil mill he designed in Wakefield. The fantail, patented a few years earlier by Edmund Lee, was first used on two mills in Wigan, one of which was a pumping mill at a local coal mine. This design had shortcomings and an improved version was devised by a millwright in Leeds, probably used first at the Leeds Pottery. The next point is the number of sails. Smeaton's recommendation was for five sails and this arrangement was first used also on the Leeds Pottery mill. Thereafter it was used on many of the mills along the Humber estuary (both industrial and corn). However, the five-sail layout did not meet with general approval from corn millers. It was certainly tried but found to have a limitation in that if one sail was damaged the mill was out of action until the sail could be repaired or replaced, whereas, with an even number of sails – four, six or eight – if one sail was damaged, the counter-balancing sail could be removed and the mill continue in operation whilst awaiting replacement. This was no doubt the approach Saunderson used, the Louth millwright who built Sibsey Trader Mill. Finally, it was the use of wind power for industrial purposes which first brought to light the need for improvement to the method of regulating sails, to compensate for changes in wind speed or power. The first practical solution was Hooper's roller sail, which initially provided a form of remote control, made self-regulating by the application of a governor. Hooper tried out his patent on two corn mills in Kent, but it was on industrial mills that they were popularised in the 1790s. The final and dominant form of self-regulating sail, which in effect is a combination of Hooper's roller sail and Meikle's spring sail, was invented by Cubitt in 1807.

Two points emerge from all this. First, in Britain it was by and large on industrial windmills that the features which combined to produce the excellent Sibsey Trader Mill were first used. It was the industrialists who were prepared to look at problems afresh, try out new ideas and take them on board. Without their involvement one might ask whether these improvements would ever have appeared.

Secondly, the few years either side of 1750 were a pivotal point in the history of millwrighting in Britain. Up to that point the evidence indicates that the English millwright was not held in particularly high regard, at least amongst industrialists. Before that date, although the original post mill may have been an English invention, all the new features in windmill design had come from

Dutch millwrights. Thereafter all the improvements to the British windmill were the result of the ingenuity of the indigenous engineers, millwrights and others, combining to produce a practical and convenient-to-use source of mechanical power. By comparison the Dutch windmill changed little during the 18th and 19th centuries.

So, to conclude, it must be accepted that during the 19th century steam power, eventually, became the dominant source of power. But the contribution of the windmill to industrial evolution should not be dismissed or ignored, and it deserves to have its contribution recorded.

Appendix 1

Summary of periods during which Industrial Windmills were built or first used

Use	1500s	1600s	1700s	1800s	1900s	Total
Oil seed		7	25	13		45
Timber trades		2	8	36		46
Mines and quarries	1	1	15	13	1	31
Paint colours			10	9		19
Whiting and cement			1	12		13
Oak bark			1	12		13
Brickworks				11		11
Saltworks			6	4		10
Snuff			7	1		8
Pottery			7	1		8
Paper			7			7
Fertiliser			1	5		6
Water supply		1	1	2	1	5
Canals			3	2		5
Lead oxide			4	2		6
Brewery etc			1	3	1	5
Textiles			2	2		4
Scutching / Rope			2	2		4
Brassworks			3			3
Miscellaneous		1	3	6	3	13
Totals	1	12	107	136	6	262

NB. Plus an unquantified number of wind engines at coal pits, salterns and brickworks

Appendix 2

List of identified windmills used for industrial purposes

The mills are listed under their county, then under the name of the nearest town or village and/or the name of the facility (if it has one). This is followed by the National Grid Reference (in brackets), the use and the earliest known date the mill was used for the specified purpose. A second date indicates the date the use ceased.

Notes

The following abbreviations are used:

    c. = circa   < = before   > = after   s = during the decade

    ? = location unknown or location uncertain or date uncertain

    * = NGR approximate   ** = NGR an indication of the general location only

    + in front of a use = added to a corn or drainage mill

Sawmill includes joiner's workshop

BEDFORDSHIRE

Husborne Crawley (SP 965 361) brickworks *c.*1800
    <1840

CAMBRIDGESHIRE

Bassingbourn [3 mills] (TL 326 436) fertiliser
    – coprolites *c.*1880 1885
Burwell (TL 591 666) fertiliser – coprolites *c.*1850
    1880s
Cambridge, Humphrey's (TL4__5__) oil seed 1820
    1845
Crowland / Spalding [several mills] (?) +oil 1696
Linton (TL 557 463) whiting *c.*1820 1929
Manea, Tidd Pratt (TL 481 902) sawmill etc *c.*1839
Melbourn (TL 35_45_) oil seed ?1770 *c.*1850
Ramsey (TL 28_ 85_) oil seed ?1770 *c.*1850
Soham, Hunts (TL 608 718) sawmill 19thC
Streetley End (TL 614 482) oak bark 1804 1820s
Wisbech (TF 464 101**) oil seed 17thC
    (TF 464 101**) oil seed <1799
    (TF 464 101**) sawmill 19thC
    Bowles (TF 464 101**) oil seed 1771 1785

CHESHIRE

Macclesfield (SJ 922 728) brassworks *c.*1770

CORNWALL

Callington, Kit's Hill (SW 375 715*) metal mine
    1848

Madron, Ding Dong Mine (SW 435 345 **) metal
    mine <1797
St Agnes (SW 725 515**) metal mine 1824
St Austell (? 2 miles outside) metal mine <1750
St Ives (SW 519 409*) +saw mill <1847 >1883
Wendron (SW 685 315**) metal mine 1711

CUMBERLAND

Cockermouth (NY 118 308) oak bark <1800
Whitehaven (NX 972 176) coal mine 1685 *c.*1715
    (NX 973 174) pottery *c.*1850
Wigton (NY 255 482) snuff *c.*1830
    (NY 254 488) oak bark *c.*1790
Workington (NY 015 288) oak bark *c.*1829

DERBYSHIRE

Ashley (SK 173 465) paint colours 1830s 1847
Derby, New Normanton (SK 352 353) lead oxide
    1792 1850s

DORSET

Poole, West Butts (SZ 008 907) scutching / rope
    *c.*1791

DURHAM

Stockton on Tees (NZ 436 196) oil seed 1786 <1794

ESSEX

Heybridge [2 mills] (TL 874 074) salt works <1825
Leyton (TQ 376 855) oil seed 1777

West Ham, Abbey Mill (TQ 388 833) oil seed 1703

GLOUCESTERSHIRE
Bath, Odd Down (ST 729 612) fuller's earth 1890
    1904
Bristol, Baptists (ST 602 744) brass works c.1754
    Clifton Down (ST 567 732) snuff 1775 1777
    Cotham (ST 576 745) snuff 1754
    Kingsweston Down (ST 547 766*) snuff 18C
    Lock's (ST 583 703) snuff <1772 c.1780
    Warmley (ST 667 727) brass works 1746
Thames Head (ST 990 985) Thames & Severn
    Canal <1789

HAMPSHIRE
Crux Easton (SU 425 563) water supply c1891
Hayling Island (SU 740 020**) salt works 18C
Lymington [several mills] (SZ 326 934**) salt works
    c.1700
Rudmore (SU 643 016) whiting <1823

KENT
Bethersden [2 mills] (TQ 929407) sawmill 19thC
Challock Lees (TR 010 520) oil seed ?19thC
Chatham (TQ 755 678*) spices
Cheriton (TR 200 374*) paper <1790
Copton (TR 014 596) water supply 1863
Deptford (?) paper c1751 1777
Dover, Buckland's (TR 308 428) brewery <1863
Eastry (TR 304 542*) oil seed <1819 >1843
Gillingham, Higgin's (TQ 784 694*) oil seed ?19thC
St Margaret's Bay (TR 363 701) electricity 1928 1939
West Farleigh (TQ 715 525**) oil seed <1889
Wormshill (TQ 876 581*) oil seed <1847

LANCASHIRE
Freckleton (SD 432 292**) sawmill 19thC
Haigh nr Wigan (SD 605 089) brewery 1845 c.1920
Lancaster (SD 467 620) paint colours 19thC
Liverpool (SJ 470 920) lead oxide <1814
    Cathedral Mount (SJ 355 894) oil seed <1723
    1805
    Dungeon (SJ 440 815*) salt works >1786
    Garston [2 mills] (SJ 405 835*) salt works 1792
    Herculaneum [2 mills] (SJ 347 882) pottery 1796
    1840
    Lime St (SJ 348 908*) oil seed c.1790
    North Shore [6 mills] (SJ 338 990**) paint
    colours <1770
    North Shore (SJ 338 990**) wood dyes <1770
    Oil St (SJ 338 917) oil seed <1832 1839
    Wapping (SJ 342 898*) salt works <1754 1790s
Manchester (SD 836 979*) wood dyes <1766
Marton Moss (SD 314 338) sawmill 19thC
Prescott, Mill Pottery (SJ 470 926) lead oxide <1814

Rimington (SD 812 449) sawmill 19thC
St Helen's (?) emery for glass polishing c.1812 1832
Wigan, Brock's Coal Mine (?SD 513 057) coal mine
    c.1749

LINCOLNSHIRE
Barrow on Humber (TA 062 229) +sawmill 1816
Barton (TA 028 231*) whiting <1804 1946
    Bank (TA 025219) whiting <1829
    Kingsforth (TA 022 189) whiting <1829 >1872
    Market Place (TA032217) whiting 1810 1815
Boston (SK 533 342) oil seed <1741 c.1800
Gainsborough (SK 815 895**) oil seed 1709 1754
    (SK 805 906) oil seed 1802
    (SK 812 889) oil seed 1826
Heckington (SK 145435) +sawmill 1830
Isle of Axholme [4 mills](SE 850 210**) oil 1657
    (SE 850 210**) gypsum 20thC
Kirton Lindsey (SK 950 986) sawmill c.1853
Louth (TM 345 882) oak bark <1840
St Peter's at Gowts (SK 973 702) oak bark <1819
Scawby (SE 987 067) oil seed 1794
    (SE 997 065) +sawmill <1822
Sutton on Sea (TF 503807) clay pit pump Late19thC
West Ferry [2 mills] (SE 808 006*) oil seed <1799

LONDON
Barking (TQ 439 829) wood dyes c.1738
Battersea (TQ 269 770) oil seed 1788 1792
Finsbury (TQ 335 823*) sawmill 1890s
Hounslow (TQ 116 741*) wood dyes 19thC
Islington [2 mills] (TQ 328 824**) lead oxide 1786
    River Head (TQ 313 828) water supply 1708
    <1720s
Lambeth (TQ 312 786) medicinal drugs <1759
    (TQ TQ 309 802) sawmill c.1658 >1760
    [2 mills] (TQ 307 800) sawmill c.1750
    Nine Elms (TQ 302 779) pottery <1762 c.1836
Limehouse (TQ 363 808**) sawmill 1633
    (TQ 363 808**) sawmill 1767 1780s
Southwark (TQ 323 803) fertiliser – bones 1790
    (TQ 317 804*) paper <1710
Wandsworth (TQ 256 748) wood dyes c.1780

NORFOLK
Ashby, Oby (TG 409 138) +sawmill 1753
Berney Arms (TG 465 049) sawmill c.1797 1821
    (TG 465 049) cement c.1856 1880
Cawston (TG 135 246) sawmill 1853
Croxton (TG 240 107) +saw mill 1842
Diss (TM 127 791) textile – spinning <1826
Drayton (TG 190 132) +sawmill <1856 <1898
Hellesden (TG 197 118) +sawmill <1826 1838
Horning, St Benet's Abbey (TG 380 157) oil seed
    c.1740 1809

King's Lynn (TF 618 206) water supply c.1698
   (?) starch 1681
   Millfleet (TF 620 197) oil seed 1680 1790s
   South (TF 621 188) oil seed 1638 1737
Norwich (TG 224 092*) oak bark <1836
   Bird's (TG 224 046) saw mill <1845
   Cann's (TG 224 043) saw mill 1850s >1883
   Carrow (TG 237 076) snuff c.1782 <1800
   Carrow (TG 237 076) textile – spinning <1800
   Gallant's (TG 243 090) sawmill 1856 1899
   Jenning's (TG 243090) sawmill c.1847 1883
Pulham Market (TM 194 866) sawmill <1825 1917
Sprowston [2 mills] (TG 240 107) sawmill <1826
   <1864 & >1864
   (TG 239 106) oak bark <1826

NORTHAMPTONSHIRE
Northampton (SP 761 604*) paper 1768 1778

NORTHUMBERLAND
Newcastle, Byker (NZ 265 648*) brickworks c.1858
   Elswick (NZ 242 631) lead oxide c.1770 c.1800
   Shield Field (NZ 457 648*) brickworks s1830
   <1856
   Stepney (NZ 260 645) oil seed 1783

NOTTINGHAMSHIRE
Sutton in Ashfield (SK 506 689) textile >1770
Wollaton (SK 525 405**) coal mine 1578

OXFORDSHIRE
Hardwick Lock (SP 464 426*) Oxford Canal 1786
Little Milton (SP 618 020) ochre 1852
South Weston (SP 703 990) ochre 19thC
Wantage (SU 340878**) oak bark 1816
Wheatley (SP 589 053) +ochre 19thC

SHROPSHIRE
Hawkstone (SJ 566 297) oil seed c.1800
Lyth Hill (SJ 470 068) scutching / rope c.1835

SOMERSET
Wellington (ST 138 205**) oak bark 19C
Wraxall (SU 490 720**) coal mine 1701

STAFFORDSHIRE
Burslem (SJ 800 159) pottery 1750 <1832
   Fountain Pottery (SJ 867 498) pottery 1780s 1800s
Etruria (SJ 868 474) pottery 1779
Werringham (SJ 942 475) coal bricks 1930 ?1940

SUFFOLK
Brandon (TL 791 862) whiting <1838 <1882
Ipswich (TM 176 453*) medicinal drugs <1804 1812
Southtown (TG 523 061*) sawmill <1825 >1844

Southwold (TM 507 759*) salt works <1839 1894
Thorpeness (TM 468 598) water supply 1924 1940
Wangford (TM 468 791) sawmill 1843 1928
Woodbridge (TM 273 493) cement 1828

SURREY
Birtley Mill (TQ 024 427*) Wey & Arun Canal 1834
   1853
Buckland (TQ 220 508) sawmill 19thC
Cranley Mill (TQ 035 402) Wey & Arun Canal 1833
   1853
Horsell Common (SU 990 596) sawmill c.1845

SUSSEX
Heathfield (TQ 585 210**) sawmill 19thC
Punnett's Town (TQ 626 209*) sawmill 1866 1933
   Cornford's (TQ 623 203) sawmill 1880s 1916

WARWICKSHIRE
Birmingham, Baskerville (SP 064 807) paper c.1748
Hutton (SP 067 895) paper 1759
Hillmorton Lock (SP 537 746**) Oxford Canal 1787
Wednesbury (?) gun barrel boring c.1725 <1754

WILTSHIRE
Devizes [2 mills] (SU 001 614) oil 1713 snuff 1740
   1784

WORCESTERSHIRE
Redditch (SP 039 675*) polishing needles c.1780
Stoke Prior (?) chemical effluent experiments 1830s

YORKSHIRE EAST
Beverley (TA 042 393) oak bark <1826
   Westwood (TA 020 382) whiting 1837 >1856
Claxton (SE 692 586) clay pit pump 19C
Elvington (SE 683 470) clay pit pump 19C
Hessle (TA 022 254) whiting c.1806 1929
Hornsea (TA 201 464) brickworks c.1866 c.1900
Howden (SE 752 311) clay pit pump ?1873
Hull, Anlaby Road (TA 085 285) oil seed 1827 >1850
   Beverley Rd (TA 090 303) paper 1796
   Cato Mill (TA101 935) oil seed c.1810 1839
   Church St, Moor's (TA 098 302) oil seed 1781
   1890s
   Church St, Pease (TA 102 302) oil seed <1719
   c.1800 (Rblt 1749)
   Dansom Lane (TA107 298) whiting <1814
   Osborne's (TA 102 300) sawmill 1798 1820s
   Salthouse Lane, Pease (TA 100 289) oil seed
   <1735 1800
   Springbank (TA 090 293) paint colours 1811
   Stoneferry (TA 10313) oil seed 1791
   Stoneferry (TA 103 312) whiting <1790 >1830
   Witham (TA 105 293) paint colours 1816

Market Weighton (TA 876 419**) oak bark 1832

Newport (SE 864 278) clay pit pump

YORKSHIRE NORTH

High Hawkser (NZ 925 076) oil seed c1868 >1915

Scarborough (TA 041 891) fertiliser – bone s1828 1840

Stakesby (NZ 448 206) oil seed 1790 1794 puddling clay late 19thC

YORKSHIRE WEST

Leeds (SE 302 322*) pottery 1772

    Brooke's (SE 370 336) oil seed 1781

Morley (SE 264 294) textile – scribbling 1787

Wakefield (SE 344 421) oil seed & wood dyes 1755

ISLE OF MAN

Ballakermeen Orchan (?) ?scutching 1780s

Billown (SC 269 702) quarry late 19thC

Kirk Michael (SC 318 907) sawmill early 19C

Ramsey (SC 445 992) +saw mill 1836 1870s

South Barrule (SC 270 768) slate quarry c.1902

WALES

Llanbadarn Fawr (SN 594 813) oak bark <1813

Llanelli, Machynus (SS 511 970) clay pit pump 1858 <1905

Anglesey, Holyhead (SK 950 986) sawmill 19thC

    Llwydiarth (SH 426 857*) brickworks c.1800 1900

    Parys Mountain (SH 443 052**) copper mine <1785 1780

    Parys Mountain (SH 444 906) copper mine 1878 >1900

    St Eilian Colour Works(SH 449 913) paint colours <1850

Clogau (SH 675 201) gold mine 19C

Garreg, Bryn Goch (SJ 136 784) lead mine <1874

Loggerheads, Cadole (SJ 203 628) lead mine 1730s 1741

Nantlle, Braich Rhydd (SH 512 548) slate quarry 1827

    Cilgwyn (SH 500 540) slate quarry 1806

    Hafod Las (SH 489 540) slate quarry c.1802 1812

Rosebush (SN 079300) quarry 19thC

Trelogan (SJ127 790**) lead mine mid-18thC

SCOTLAND

Airth (NS 900 880**) sawmill <1723

Balgonie (ST 300 990**) coal mine 1732

Bo'ness and Carridon (NT 013815) coal mine c1750

Broughty Castle (NO 465 310*) sawmill <1855 1878

Dunbar (NT 702763) quarry <1853

Edinburgh (NT 260 720**) brewery <1768

Glasgow, Westmuir (NS 700 700**) coal mine 1737 1740

Kirkcudbright (NX 687501) cider press

Leith (NT 208 770**) grinding & refining lead ore <1703

Marykirk (?) electricity 1887 1906

Olrig (ND 195685) flagstone quarry <1873

Peterhead, Glenugie (NK 125442) distillery 1822

St Monans, Lord Kellie (NO 534 420) coal mine c.1746

St Monans (NO 534019) salt works 1772

Stoneykirk (NX 095522) scutching <1847

Strathore (ST 209 960**) coal mine c.1738

Strathspey (NJ 341 655*) sawmill 1786

Thurso (ND 075676) flagstone quarry <1872

Bibliography of Sources

Abbreviations used:

IAR   Industrial Archaeology Review
SPAB   Society for the Preservation of Ancient Buildings
TIMS   The International Molinological Society
TNS   Transactions of the Newcomen Society

Anderson, M.L., *A History of Scottish Forestry*, Nelson 1967

Angerstein, *Illustrated Travel Diary 1753-1755* (translated by Torsten and Peter Berg), Science Museum 2001

Annison, R. and Chapman, L., *The Hawes Ropemaker*, pub by authors 1983

Apling, H., *Norfolk Corn Mills*, The Norfolk Windmill Trust (Norwich) 1984

Ashton, T.S., *The Industrial Revolution 1760-1830*, OUP 1948

Barton, D.B., *The Cornish Beam Engine*, Pitman Press (Bath) 1969

Bawden, T.A. *et al.*, *Industrial Archaeology of the Isle of Man*, David & Charles (Newton Abbot) 1972

Beard, F., *On and About Lyth Hill*, 1987

Bennet, R. and Elton, J., *History of Corn Milling*, Simpkin, Marshall & Co. 1898/1904

Brace, H.W., 'Seed Crushing in Gainsborough', *Lincolnshire Architecture and Archaeological Society Reports and Papers Vol VI 2*, 1956

Brace, H.W., *History of Seed Crushing in Great Britain*, Land Books Ltd 1960

Brunnarius, M., *The Windmills of Sussex*, Phillimore 1979

Buckland, J.S.P., 'John Smeaton's Windmill Designs', *Procs of the 2nd Mills Research Conference*, 1984

Buckland, J.S.P., *Lee's Patent Windmill 1744-1747*, SPAB 1987

Buckland, J.S.P., 'The Punnett's Town, Heathfield, Wind Saw Mills', *Sussex Industrial History No 21*, 1991

Calvert, N.G., *Windpower Principles: their application on the small scale*, Charles Griffin & Co. Ltd 1979

Campbell, W.A., *The Chemical Industry*, Longman 1871

Chaloner, W.H., 'Charles Roe of Macclesfield (1715-81): an Eighteenth-Century Industrialist', *Trans of the Lancashire and Cheshire Antiquarian Society*, 1950/51

Clark, A., *Windmill Land*, W. Foulsham & Co. Ltd 1923

Coles Finch, W., *Watermills and Windmills*, Arthur Cassell (Sheerness) 1993

Cooper, E.R., 'A Note of the Saltpans in Suffolk', *TNS XIX* 1938/9

Copeland, R., *A Short History of Pottery Raw Materials and the Cheddleton Flint Mill*, Cheddleton Flint Mill Industrial Heritage Trust (Leek) 1972

Craven, M., *Derby. An Illustrated History*, Breedon Books (Derby) 1988

D'acres, R., *The Art of Water-Drawing*, The Newcomen Society 1930

Darby, H.C., *The Changing Fenland*, CUP 1985

Day, J., *Bristol Brass*, David & Charles (Newton Abbot) 1973

Deane, P., *The First Industrial Revolution*, CUP 2nd ed. 1979

Defoe, D., *A Tour Through the Whole Island of Great Britain*, Dent 1962

Dolman, P., *Lincolnshire Windmills, a contemporary survey*, Lincolnshire County Council 1986

Donaldson, J., *The Roller Mill & Silo Manual*, Northern Publishing Co. Ltd 4th ed. 1921

Douch, H.L., *Cornish Windmills*, Oscar Blackford Ltd (Truro) n.d.

Douglas, G. *et al.*, *Scottish Windmills: A Survey*, Scottish Industrial Archaeology Survey 1984

Douglas, G. and Oglethorpe, M., 'Scottish Windpower and Windmills, New Information', *IAR IX No 1*, Autumn 1986

Duckham, Baron F., *A History of the Scottish Coal Industry*, Vol.1, David & Charles (Newton Abbot) 1970

Earnshaw, J.R., 'The Site of a Medieval Post Mill at Bridlington', *Yorkshire Archaeological Journal Vol 45*, 1973

Enfield, W., *An Essay towards the History of Liverpool*, Warrington 1773

Evans, H., 'Wedgwood, Windmills and Water Power', *Procs of the Wedgwood Society No.8*, 1970

Farey, J., *A Treatise on the Steam Engine*, David & Charles (Newton Abbot) 1971

Farries, K.G., *Essex Windmills. Millers and Millwrights, Vol 3*, Charles Skilton & Co. 1984

Farries, K.G. and Mason, M.T., *The Windmills of Surrey and Inner London*, Charles Skilton & Co. 1966

Fergus, D., 'Windmills Turning in my Dreams', *Scotts Magazine*, March 1966

Filby, P., 'The Smock Mill in Cambridgeshire: An Historical Survey', *Procs of the 15th Mills Research Conference*, 1999

Flint, B., *Suffolk Windmills*, The Boydell Press (Woodbridge) 1979

Foreman, W., *Oxfordshire Mills*, Phillimore 1983

Gifford, A., *Derbyshire Windmills*, Midlands Wind & Water Mills Group 1995

Gillett, E., *History of Grimsby*, Hull University Press 1970

Greenhill, F.A., 'Old Windmill at Broughty Ferry', *Procs Scottish Archaelogical Society LXXV*, 1950/51

Greenslade, M.W. and Stuart, D.G., *A History of Staffordshire*, Phillimore 1998

Gregory, R., *East Yorkshire Windmills*, Charles Skilton Ltd 1985

Gregory, R., 'The Use of Power in the Early Industrial Development of Hull', *IAR Vol XV No.1*, 1992

Guise, B. and Lees, G., *Windmills of Anglesey*, Attic Books (Wales) 1992

Hadfield, C., *The Canals of the East Midlands*, David & Charles (Newton Abbot) 1966

Hansen, M. and Waterfield, J., *Boston Windmills*, G.W. Belron Ltd (Gainsborough) 1995

Harris, T.R., 'Engineering in Cornwall before 1775', *TNS XXV*, 1945/7

Harrison, J.K., *Eight Centuries of Milling in North East Yorkshire*, North Yorkshire National Parks Authority 2001

Head, S.G., *A Home Tour through the Manufacturing Districts of England in the Summer of 1835*, Frank Cass & Co. 2nd ed 1968

Hesleden, W.S., *A Sketch of the Properties and Advantages of Sutton's Gravitated Sails for Windmills*, pub by the Author 1807

Hillen, H.J., *History of Kings Lynn*, 1907, EP Publishing (Wakefield) reprint 1978

Hills, R.L., *Papermaking in Britain 1588-1988*, The Athlone Press 1988

Hills, R.L., *Power from the Wind*, CUP 1994

Honey, W.B., *English Pottery and Porcelain*, Adam & Charles Black 1949

Hoskins, W.G., *The Making of the English Landscape*, Penguin Books 1955

Household, H., *The Thames and Severn Canal*, David & Charles (Newton Abbot) 1969

Howes, H., *Bedfordshire Mills*, Bedfordshire County Council 1983

Hughes, G.N., 'Wind, Water and Animal Powered Mills and Gins in Prescott, SW Lancs 1453-1908', *Wind and Watermills North West Review No.9*, 1994

Hughes, J., 'Cumberland Windmills', *Trans of the Cumberland and Westmorland Antiquarian and Archaeological Socierty Vol LXXII New Series*, 1972

Jackson, G., *The History and Archaeology of Ports*, World's Work (Todworth) 1983

Jarvis, P.S., *Stability in Windmills*, TIMS 1981

Job, B., *Staffordshire Windmills*, Midland Wind and Watermills Group 1985

Job, B., *Watermills of the Moddershall Valley*, 1994

John, A.H. (ed.), *The Walker Family, Iron Founders and Lead Manufacturers 1741-1893*, CPBA 1951

Jones, P.A. and Simmons, E.H., *The Story of the Saw*, Spear and Jackson 1961

Kelly, N., 'Manx Windmills. A Contemporary Survey', *Procs of the 12th Mills Research Conference*, 1995

Kidson, J.R. and F., *Historical Notices of Leeds Pottery*, SR Publishers Ltd (Wakefield) 1970

Kilburn Scott, E., 'Early Cloth Fulling and its Machinery', *TNS XII*, 1931/2

Lancaster Burne, E., 'On Mills, by Thomas Telford', *TNS XVII*, 1926/7

Lewis, J. *et al.*, *The Salt and Coal Industries at St Monan's Fife in the 18th and 19th Centuries*, Tayside & Fife Archaeological Committee (Glenrothen) 1999

Lloyd, A.T., 'The Salterns of the Lymington Area', *Procs of the Hampshire Field Club and Archaeological Society*, 1967

Longley, K.M., 'Origin of the Smock Mill', *TNS XLI*, 1968-69

Lord, E., *Derby Past*, Phillimore 1996

Lord, J., *Capital & Steam Power*, 2nd ed. Frank Cass 1966 [1st ed. 1923]

McKenna, J., 'Birmingham Windmills', *Trans of the Birmingham and Warwickshire Archaeological Society for 1983-2 Vol.93*

Major, J.K., 'An Inventory of Windmills in Northumberland and Durham', *Industrial Archaeology Vol IV No.4*, Nov 1867

Mathias, P., *The First Industrial Nation*, Methuen & Co. Ltd 2nd ed. 1983

Matkin, 'John Rennie's Diary of a Journey through Northern England 1784', *Historical Study No.2*, East Kent Maritime Trust

Meteyard, E., *The Life and Works of Wedgwood* (?) 1865

Nash, G., 'An Introduction to the Windmills of Wales', *TIMS Trans of the 6th Symposium*, 1985

Pardoe, F.E., *John Baskerville of Birmingham: Letter-Founder & Printer*, Frederick Muller Ltd 1875

Parker, V., *The Making of King's Lynn*, Phillimore 1971

Paterson, D.S., 'Two Wind Saw Mills in Lancashire', *SPAB Wind and Watermill Section Newsletter No.67*, 1996

Paterson, D.S., 'Industrial Mills in Lancashire', *North West Review*, 1999

Prentis, W.H., *The Snuff Mill Story* (Mitcham) 1970

Proctore, R.W., *Memorials of Manchester Streets*, Thomas Sutcliffe (Manchester) 1874

Pyne, W.H., *Delineation of the Arts, Crafts, Manufactures etc of Great Britain*, 1808

Reynolds, T.S., *Stronger than a Hundred Men*, The John Hopkins UP 1983

Richards, A.J., *The Slate Quarries of Pembrokeshire*, Carreg Gwalch 1998

Richards, A.J., *A Gazetteer of the Welsh Slate Industry*, Carreg Gwalch 1991

Rodenhurst, T., *A Description of Hawkstone, the Seat of Sir Richard Hill, Bart.*, John Stockdale 6th ed. 1799

Seaby, W.A. and Smith, A.C., *Windmills in Shropshire, Hereford and Worcester*, Stevenage Museums 1984

Scott, E.K., 'Smeaton's Engine of 1767 at New River Head, London', *TNS XIX*, 1938/0

Sharpe, A., *A Brief History of the Morley Textile Industry*, Morley Local History Society 1968

Shaw, S., *History of the Staffordshire Potteries*, 1829, David & Charles reprint

Sheahan, J.J., *History of the Town of Kingston upon Hull*, John Green (Beverley) 2nd ed. 1866

Short, M., *Windmills in Lambeth*, London Borough of Lambeth 1971

Shorter, A.H., *Water Paper Mills in England*, SPAB 1966

Simond, L., *An American in Regency England*, Robert Maxwell 1968

Singer, S. *et al.*, *History of Technology*, Vol.IV, OUP 1966

Skempton, A.W. (ed.), *John Smeaton FRS*, Thomas Telford Ltd 1981

Smith, A., *Drainage Windmills of the Norfolk Marshes*, Stevenage Museums 1990

Smith, D., *Water-Supply and Public Health Engineering*, Ashgate (Aldershot) 1999

Smith, R.S., *Early Coal-mining around Nottingham 1500-1650*, University of Nottingham 1989

Stainwright, T.L., *Windmills of Northamptonshire*, W.D. Wharton (Wellingborough) 1991

Stokhuyzen, F., *The Dutch Windmill*, Merlin Press 1962

Stokhuyzen, F., *Molens*, Fibula-Van Dishevck (Harlem) 1981

Tann, J., 'Boulton & Watt Engines', *TNS IL*, 1977/8

Thomas, J., 'Josiah Wedgwood as a Pioneer of Steam Power in the Pottery Industry', *TNS XVII*, 1936/7

Tickell, J., *History of the Town and County of Kingston upon Hull*, Brown (Hull) 1798

Trigg, A., *The Windmills of Hampshire*, Milestone Publications (Horndean) n.d.

Tyson, B., 'Two Post Mills at Whitehaven in the Seventeenth Century', *Trans Cumberland and Westmorland Antiquarian and Archaeological Society Vol.LXXXVIII*, 1988

Uglow, J., *The Lunar Men*, Faber & Faber 2001

Vine, P.A.L., *London's Lost Route to the Sea*, David & Charles (Newton Abbot) 1965

Wailes, R., 'Lincolnshire Windmills Part II Tower Mills', *TNS XXIX*, 1953/55

Wailes, R., 'Notes on the Windmill Drawings in Smeaton's Designs', *TNS XXVIII*, 1961/3

Wailes, R., 'Water-driven Mills for Grinding Stone', *TNS XXXIX*, 1966/7

Wailes, R., *The English Windmill*, Routledge & Kegan Paul 1954

Ward, N., *There's no place like ... Morley*, The Ridings Publishing Co (Driffield) 1980

Ward, O., 'The Odd Down Windmill', *Trans TIMS Tenth Symposium*, 1992

Watts, M. and Coulthard, A.J., *Windmills of Somerset*, The Research Publishing Co. 1980

Watts, M., *Wiltshire Windmills*, Wiltshire Library & Museum Service 1980

West, J., *The Windmills of Kent*, Skilton & Shaw 1979

Young, A., *A General View of the Agriculture of the County of Lincolnshire*, Sherwood, Neely & Jones 1813

Zyl, J. van, *Moolen-Boek*, Amsterdam 1761

Harry Apling Notes – Unpublished research notes held by Norfolk Windmills Trust

H.E. Simmons Notes – Unpublished research notes and photographs held by the Science Museum Library and the National Monuments Record

Boulton & Watt Archive – Birmingham Central Library

Index

Page numbers in **bold** refer to illustrations